Shiny Sheff

The Story of Sheffield's Fighting Ships

by

Alistair Lofthouse

ALD Design & Print

Published and Printed by:
ALD Design & Print
279 Sharrow Vale Road
Sheffield S11 8ZF
Great Britain

Telephone: 0114 268 6269

ISBN: 1-901587-03-7

First Published June 1998

Other titles in the series:

Mi-Amigo - The Story of Sheffield's Flying Fortress - David Harvey ISBN 1-901587-00-2
Tales From a Peak District Bookshop - Mike Smith   ISBN 1-901587-01-0
Tha' Don't Look Proper - Anne Hunt   ISBN 1-901587-02-9

Foreword

In February 1997 the printers and publishers, ALD Design & Print, launched the book *Mi-Amigo - The Story of Sheffield's Flying Fortress*. Extensively researched by local historian David Harvey, the book tells the touching story of a young American B-17 crew that were tragically killed when their lost and crippled aircraft crashed in a Sheffield city park. Miraculously, children playing nearby survived unhurt.

Some months after the book was launched I was in the central branch of W.H.Smith looking at the local history books. It struck me that, although there were plenty of books concerning Sheffield trams, the two local football teams and the extensive history of Sheffield's industry, there was not one single book about the *Shiny Sheffs*, Sheffield's fighting ships.*

The idea then came that it might be a good idea for someone to write a book about Sheffield's naval connections, bringing the events, history, successes and losses to the people of Sheffield.

A few days later I discussed this on the telephone with Martin Dawes of the Sheffield Star. Whilst reading the Sheffield Star the next day I discovered that it was myself who was to write this book!

I have been overwhelmed by the assistance received by former sailors of *HMS Sheffields*, without whom this book would be only half the book that it is.

I do accept the viewpoint of some of Sheffield's veterans that the country they fought for is not what it was, but considering that the author is 31 years old, they can be reassured that there is a considerable percentage of today's new generation who, not only take an interest in what their grandfathers' generation did, but also appreciate their sacrifice and suffering.

I was concerned a few months ago, when some promised photographs from a wartime sailor didn't arrive. When they did eventually arrive I was touched by the remarks at the end of his letter: "Sorry about the delay in sending you the photographs. Since I've retired I just don't know where I found the time to go to work. It's a brilliant life."

Alistair Lofthouse

* In 1988 Ronald Basset wrote an excellent account of the first *HMS Sheffield's* wartime exploits. It is now, however, out of print.

Acknowledgements

I am extremely grateful to the following people for their information and loan of their personal photographs and records: *Vic Chappel, Jim Cordy, Tony Cooke, Ann Diver, John Dean, Brian Dunk, Sydney Greenwood, Denis King, Norman Lane, Tim Robinson, A.E.Richardson, D.Ramshall, Commander Stanley Walker, Bob Mahoney, B.Briscoe, Mr Drew, Commander Mike Norman AFC, OBE and James McMinnis.*

Line drawings of the three *HMS Sheffields* and *Cadmus: J.Morris.*

The HMS Sheffield Association, especially *Ken Burkinshaw*, General Secretary, for allowing unlimited access to their records and photographs.

Sheffield Newspapers for allowing access to their archives and their librarian, *Susan Woods*, for assistance in addition to her normal duties.

The Imperial War Museum for access to their records and photographs.

The Navy News for publishing my request for information.

BBC Radio Sheffield for their interest.

Lieutenant Tennuci and *Commander Colin Hamp* of the current *HMS Sheffield.*

The Ministry of Defence for clearance to use photographs and allowing free use of any pre-1948 pictures.

On the production side: *Simon Dawson* Assistant Researcher, *Andrew Billingham* Text and Technical Editor, *Elizabeth Mottram* administration and painting of 'The Battle of Barents Sea'.

Encouragement, even in the darkest hours: *David Harvey.*

Fold out plan of *Old Shiny* © *Alistair Lofthouse*, based on drawings from The HMS Sheffield Association.

Photograph references: H.M.S.S.A. - HMS Sheffield Association, R.N. - Royal Navy, I.W.M. - Imperial War Museum, M.P.L. - Maritime Picture Library, Crown Copyright /MOD - Reproduced with the permission of Her Majesty's Stationery Office.

Front cover: Ship's crest: Crown Copyright/MOD, Photos (in order of appearance) Ann Diver, H.M.S.SA, Crown Copyright/MOD.

Rear cover: Photos (in order of appearance) Sheffield Newspapers, Crown Copyright/MOD, I.W.M.

Contents

Battle Honours of HMS Sheffield

Norway	1940
Spartivento	1940
Atlantic	1941-43
Bismarck	1941
Mediterranean	1941
Malta Convoys	1941
Arctic	1941-43
North Africa	1942
Barents Sea	1942
Salerno	1943
Biscay	1943
North Cape	1943
Falkland Islands	1982

The HMS Sheffield Association

Have you served on any of the *HMS Sheffields* ?

The HMS Sheffield Association is open to anyone, regardless of rank, who has served on *HMS Sheffield*.

The Association has regular meetings and newsletters and would like to hear from you.

Please contact:

Ken Burkinshaw, General Secretary
HMS Sheffield Association
132 Cherry Tree Street
Barnsley   S74 9RG
UK

In Memory of

B. Brooks	D. George	A. Ling
J. Marjoram	A. Nedwill	J. Penn
J. Saville	A. Spong	A. C. Taylor
F. W. Wint		

1940-42

D. Balfour	D. Briggs	M.Chappel
D. Cope	A. Eggington	R. Emly
R. Fagan	N. Goodhall	C.Keng
A. Knowles	A. Marshall	A. Norman
D. Osborne	K. Sullivan	A. Swallow
M. Till	B. Wallis	A. Wellstead
B. Welsh	K. Williams	J. Woodhead

1982

In The Beginning - 1937

The City of Sheffield was late in having a fighting ship. Nottingham's first ship was built in 1703, London's first 'man of war' in 1636 and Newcastle's first dated from 1653. But it was not until July 23rd 1936 that the first *HMS Sheffield* slipped into the Tyne at 6.30pm, launched by Her Royal Highness Princess Marina, Duchess of Kent.

HMS Sheffield was one of ten 'Town Class' light cruisers that were being rapidly built as part of Britain's re-armament, in anticipation of the forthcoming hostility with Germany. Her sister ships were the *Southampton, Newcastle, Glasgow, Birmingham, Manchester, Liverpool, Gloucester, Belfast* and *Edinburgh.*

As the first to be completed was the *Southampton,* all the ships tended to be referred to as the *'Southampton Class'.* Their design was developed from previous classes of British cruisers, but the class was to excel itself in the coming conflicts and remains today the most famous class of cruiser.

HMS Sheffield was to become a special ship due to her affiliation with the City of Sheffield.

Princess Marina arrives to launch the first HMS Sheffield (Photo: H.M.S.S.A)

Sheffield slides down the slipway into the Tyne July 23rd 1936 (Photo: H.M.S.S.A)

All her fittings that would normally be made of brass were made of stainless steel, a corrosion resistant, shiny steel with a high chromium content, discovered in Sheffield by Harry Brearley in 1913. These items included railings, staghorns and even the ship's bell. The Royal Navy thought that this trial was worthwhile in order to see if stainless steel would reduce the amount

New stainless steel items on Sheffield; a staghorn (Photo: Norman Lane) and ship's crest (Photo: H.M.S.S.A).

of work required by the crew in cleaning the brassware. In fact, her bell was the first stainless steel bell to be fitted to a ship and was made by *Hadfields* of Sheffield, where Meadowhall Shopping Centre now stands. It was the first bell they had ever made. *Hadfields* were more used to producing railway track, tin hats and armour piercing shells.

*At 17:00 hrs on August 25th 1937 the Civilian Red Ensign
was lowered, the White Ensign hoisted and thus the name
Sheffield graced a Royal Navy warship for the first time*
(Photo: H.M.S.S.A)

Another first for the *Sheffield* was that she was the first ship in the Royal Navy to have radar or, as it was known pre-war, **ra**dio **d**irection **a**nd **r**anging equipment. Indeed, as war neared, the only other ship in the Navy with radar was the battleship *Rodney.*

The ladies of Sheffield present their handmade Ensign (behind) (Photo: H.M.S.S.A)

Sheffield contributed more than just stainless steel to *HMS Sheffield.* The ladies of the city provided a silk Union Jack and a silver and white Ensign to the ship. These flags were flown every time the vessel went into combat. Now they hang in Sheffield Cathedral. Also many other Sheffield City companies gave cutlery, coasters, silver tankards and paintings.

Gifts and silverware all from Sheffield companies (Photo: H.M.S.S.A)

The *'Shiny Sheff'*, as she became affectionately known, had been launched without her guns, superstructure, funnels, masts and electrics. It took thirteen months to complete the ship and on Wednesday August 25th 1937, the White Ensign was hoisted and Captain W. Mark-Wardlaw accepted the first *HMS Sheffield* from her builder, *Vickers-Armstrong* of Newcastle and set sail for Chatham on the Thames, the ship's new base.

Chief Stoker Tom Bolton opens up Sheffield for the first time. Bolton was the first crewman to board Sheffield in 1936 and, by special arrangement, he was the last to leave her in 1967 (Photo: H.M.S.S.A)

Sheffield spent the next few months 'working up', getting the new crew used to their new ship. On October 13th 1937 she visited Immingham near Hull so that the people of Sheffield could visit their new ship and the ship's company could visit the city they represented. Over the three days that the ship was open to the public, she was visited by over 20,000 people and, in return, around two hundred of the ship's company came to Sheffield to watch Sheffield United play Sheffield Wednesday at Hillsborough. Wednesday won 1-0.

Sheffield's crew and band marching on to the pitch at Hillsborough (Photo: H.M.S.S.A)

In the evening a dance was organised for the sailors at the Town Hall. Two hundred girls were carefully selected by a committee of Sheffield ladies. It is reported in the ship's records that the sailors were disappointed at this event because the girls were chosen for their virtue and the crew, being young sailors, expected something different!

After this introduction to the City of Sheffield, *HMS Sheffield* joined the Home Fleet. The Home Fleet tended, as the name suggests, to spend most of its time around the United Kingdom. However, it did spend a few months a year in the Mediterranean exercising with the Royal Navy's Mediterranean fleet. *Sheffield* visited Gibraltar and Tangier in her first year of service.

The new Sheffield seen from a bi-plane, probably at Chatham Naval Base (Photo: H.M.S.S.A)

In July of 1938, back in the UK, *Sheffield's* first captain left to be replaced by Captain E de F Renauf CVO and it was during this time that John Logie Baird, inventor of the television, visited *Sheffield* to examine her new radar which could spot aircraft up to forty miles away. The scanner was located on the fore-mast and was nicknamed the cuckoo's nest by the crew due to its unusual appearance.

Sheffield was also making her name known within the fleet at sport. Her crew beat every opponent in 'tug of war' culminating with a record of 21 minutes pull with her sister ship *Southampton's* crew at Gibraltar.

A famous picture of Sheffield under way pre-war (Photo: Sheffield Newspapers)

On one occasion whilst at Gibraltar fifty of *Sheffield's* crew visited the German pocket battleship, *Graf Spee*, at anchor in the bay. The *Graf Spee* scuttled herself after the Battle of the River Plate in 1939.

Sheffield during the Spanish Civil War. Stripes have been painted across the gun turrets to identify the ship as British (Photo: J. McMinnis)

Unofficial ship's mascot. Warships such as Sheffield would carry one or two cats to catch any vermin
(Photo: J. Cordy)

The War Years
The Making of a Legend

As war broke out, the first *HMS Sheffield* was patrolling the North Atlantic in a position some two hundred miles due south of Iceland. The crew didn't know what to expect: Would there be a great German breakout? Would the Luftwaffe attack? In the end, not much happened. This was a stage of the war known as the 'Phoney War'.

Physical training, 1939 style, at Scapa Flow (Photo: H.M.S.S.A)

For the *Sheffield,* her first encounter with the enemy occurred on October 20th 1939, when she came across the German freighter *Gloria* near to Norway. No shots were fired but a British 'prize crew' boarded the *Gloria* to sail her to the safety of Kirkwall in the Orkneys. *Old Shiny* spent the next four months patrolling the North Atlantic, an exhausting, cold, wet and dull job.

Gloria, captured by Old Shiny, 1939 (Photo: J.Cordy)

At the beginning of 1940 *Sheffield* gained her third captain, Charles Larcom, and on January 19th she suffered her first casualty. A young sailor, John Penn, was thrown overboard in heavy seas and was never seen again.

Germany invaded Norway on April 7th so *Sheffield* headed north with her sister ships *Glasgow, Manchester* and *Southampton* along with the battleship *Rodney*. The mission seemed poorly planned. The British were bombed by German Stuka dive bombers and withdrew. Fortunately damage was minimal, but a lesson was rapidly learned: British ships could not operate near enemy coastlines without air support.

As *Sheffield* withdrew to Scapa Flow the Luftwaffe struck again with a raid of around sixty aircraft. The raid lasted an hour, six attackers were downed and no vessels were hit.

The whole Norwegian campaign was a shambles. *Sheffield* and *Glasgow* returned to Norway on April 14th. At Namsos, ninety miles north of Trondheim, they landed a force of some two hundred of their crew, including stokers and other non-fighting trained men, armed with First World War rifles, with the intention of fighting off crack German paratrooper units. Equipped with gear from the 1914-18 war, what could young stokers do against well-trained, well-equipped soldiers? Fortunately three days later, rather cold and hungry, the sailors returned to the warmth of their ship.

Sheffield returned again to Norway on April 22nd, this time with her aircraft hangars loaded with guns and trucks for the army, along with around seven hundred soldiers. These reinforcements were bound for Molde, south of Trondheim, to continue the liberation of Norway. However, events were not going well. With dreadful weather, no air cover and poorly equipped troops, the British counter attack failed. By April 28th *Sheffield* was evacuating British troops and Norwegians from the advancing Germans. One of these evacuees was only a few hours old!

Norway 1940 (Photo: J.Cordy)

Iceland 1940 (Photo: J.Cordy)

During May a German invasion of Britain was anticipated so *Old Shiny* was kept at readiness, anchored off Immingham ready to attack the invasion fleet.

On June 9th Italy declared war on Britain. *Sheffield's* paintwork had been changed from all over grey to camouflage shades of grey and blue. The concept was not to hide the ship but to make identification harder.

The Phoney War was over now and *Sheffield* docked for ten days of repairs. The crew had nine days leave before *Old Shiny* was off to pastures new, but no-one was told where.

Force H From Gibraltar

Sheffield was to start the most famous part of her career. She would join Force H, the name given to a fleet of Royal Navy ships based at Gibraltar, under the command of Vice Admiral Sir James Somerville.

Other elements in the force were aircraft carrier *Ark Royal* and the battle cruiser *Renown.* Italy's entrance into the war would mean an enlarged role for Force H and *Old Shiny's* new radar would come in handy. However *Sheffield's* sailors were unaware of the importance of their deployment. At this time radar was still secret.

Force H had two main roles: firstly to defend convoys in and out of the western Mediterranean and, secondly, to attack and be a 'thorn in the Italians' side'.

The convoys, or as 'Jamie' Somerville called them 'club rooms', had two purposes: to get essential supplies of food to the people of Malta and to supply military equipment to allied forces on Malta and the eastern Mediterranean.

Admiral Cunningham had his fleet, Force F, based in Malta. Upon Italy joining the war he'd had to move his major units to Alexandria, Egypt to be safe from air attack.

One of *Sheffield's* early operations with Force H was 'Smash and Grab'. In order to get reinforcements of warships to Admiral Cunningham, Force H would undertake a diversionary raid. The diversion would keep the Italians busy while Cunningham's new ships passed close to enemy held land, such as Sicily and Libya.

Somerville's diversion would involve *Old Shiny*, the battle cruiser *Renown,* the aircraft carrier *Ark Royal* and seven destroyers. *Ark Royal's* aircraft would bomb the target at the port of Caylians, the capital of Sardinia. This was Operation 'Smash' and Operation 'Grab' consisted of destroyers sailing near Baleain and sending false radio reports to convince the Italians that Cunningham's ships were five hundred miles away from where they actually

*The three members of Force H: The flagship battle cruiser Renown (front),
aircraft carrier Ark Royal (middle) and cruiser Sheffield in the distance*
(Photo: R.N.)

were. In the event the air raid was of only limited success, but with no British casualties. Cunningham's force through the mission had been a success.

On February 6th 1942 Vice Admiral Somerville in *Renown* lead Force H out of Gibraltar for what was probably one of the most audacious operations of the war.

Old Shiny, *The Ark* and the old battleship *Malaya* followed *Renown*. As normal *Sheffield's* crew knew nothing of their mission except that they were off to the Mediterranean for something to do with Italian shipping.

At tea time Force H passed Ibiza and Majorca off the coast of Spain. By morning they were in sight of Nice and Monte Carlo. They were heading for the Gulf of Genoa, but why?

It was Monday morning just before 06:00 hours when the answer came. *Sheffield, Renown* and *Malaya* were to bombard the Italian port of Genoa. In particular they were after the shipyard and the docks.

From ten miles away in the mist of dawn the force of three opened fire on the unsuspecting Italian town. For twenty minutes the enemy thought that they were subject to bombing from aircraft. *Sheffield's* Walrus aircraft were 10,000 feet above Genoa attracting some anti-aircraft fire.

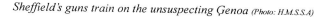

Sheffield's guns train on the unsuspecting Genoa (Photo: H.M.S.S.A)

All Italian guns had been firing skyward until they realised that the attack was from the sea. The surprise was total and by the time Italian coastal guns were firing the British had departed.

Paint is blistered on Sheffield's guns after the bombardment (Photo: J.Cordy)

Meanwhile *Ark Royal's* aircraft had attacked La Spezia, Livorna and Pisa.

Italian revenge took place at 10:00. As Force H was on the run, a few bombers made a vain attack on *Ark Royal* but their bombs missed by literally a mile. Rome radio later claimed that *Sheffield* had been sunk during the raid.

After the bombardment empty shell cases litter the deck (Photo: J.Dean)

Force H, including *Old Shiny*, was back home at Gibraltar on February 11th having suffered no casualties or damage.

H.M.S Sheffield had fired 782 high explosive shells during the raid. 28 merchant ships were either sunk or damaged during the raid and much of Genoa's dock and shipyard were damaged.

Old Shiny follows The Ark and Renown home (Photo: H.M.S.S.A)

October 8th 1940, one of Sheffield's Walrus aircraft has landed after an anti-submarine patrol. The man on the wing is about to hook up the seaplane to the ship's crane

As the aircraft is being lifted clear a wave hits it and the hook breaks plunging the Walrus into the sea.

The man is thrown clear as the engine is still running

Beyond salvage the Walrus has to be finished off by Sheffield's anti-aircraft guns (Photos: J.Cordy)

The Battle of Spartivento

The Malta convoy runs were the first concern of Force H. With the reinforcements in aircraft, men and ammunition that reached the beleaguered island from the west, its fate hung no less surely than on the hard-fought help that reached it from the east.

The following battle description is based on an eye-witness account.

On November 11th the Eastern Mediterranean Fleet had carried out the brilliant attack on Taranto, Italy. Though the damage inflicted by the ancient Swordfish of the Fleet Air Arm was temporary, its effects, both immediate and ultimate, on the balance of power in the Mediterranean were overwhelming.

The White Ensign made by the ladies of Sheffield is raised for battle (Photo: H.M.S.S.A)

A fortnight later the Admiralty had ships at Gibraltar ready to exploit the opportunity that the Swordfish had created.

At dawn on November 25th, reinforced Force H sailed in bad weather from the Rock. The force now consisted of *Renown, Ark Royal, Sheffield, Southampton, Manchester,* and *Dispatch,* with eight destroyers. The task was to force a fast convoy through the narrows with urgent supplies for the Army of the Western Desert.

The opening phase of the operation differed in no way from the runs that had been made before. At 09:00 on the 27th the convoy was closed up to take up cruising positions. At 09:23 the British intercepted an aircraft signal reporting the presence of enemy warships. They were

75 miles roughly north-east form the convoy. Somerville ordered his fast cruisers, including *Sheffield,* to sail at full speed to attack the Italians. At three minutes past noon a single mast and smoke were sighted due north of *Old Shiny*. The flags broke at the mastheads for the signal 'enemy in sight'.

The story of the Battle of Spartivento is a strange, exhilarating mixture of failure and reckless courage.

A Walrus was launched at 12:30 to give directions to the gunners of *Renown*. The larger Italian guns were throwing down accurate fire before *Sheffield* could engage. Scarcely had the flags signalled the enemy than a lookout reported aircraft astern. *Ark Royal* was out of sight in a waiting position below the horizon. She had launched her Swordfish bi-planes to attempt to torpedo the Italians from the air.

Sister ship Manchester, seen from Sheffield with a near miss off her port bow
(Photo: J.Cordy)

There was a little fine weather cloud about. The aircraft disappeared behind a small white patch and reappeared again almost at once. The cloud was not enough to hide their approach and they were going in against the whole weight of the Italian fleet.

Rapidly the mastheads and the smoke smudges on the horizon grew into ships. The Italians could be seen stretched out in a vast line across the horizon. The brand new battleship *Vittorio Veneto* appeared and then the *Guilio Cesare*, then more 8 inch cruisers and sixteen destroyers.

The cruisers *Sheffield, Manchester, Newcastle* and *Southampton,* with the old *Berwick* in support, formed a line of bearing and headed at maximum speed towards the enemy.

Far behind, the old battleship *Ramillies* was struggling to catch up on the horizon, with her old First World War boilers at bursting point. *Renown,* coming along well, was still out of range. The five cruisers were on their own.

The four sister ships acted as one. *Renown* came within range and opened fire. Her first salvos were dreadful. Then, as she found the range, she ran a bearing on one propeller shaft and slowly, inexorably fell away astern of the battle group.

Ark Royal surrounded by water spray from near misses (Photo: R.N.)

Sheffield and the other cruisers went on headlong towards the enemy, maintaining a rate of fire that kept the horizon between and around the enemy ships forested with plumes of spray.

Then, well away from the spray, spout puffballs of black smoke could be seen moving in closer and closer towards the heavy ships. The Swordfish were going in to the attack through a clear sky and in the perfect noonday visibility. The Italian heavy ships were now firing and the cruisers altered course to reduce the range.

Berwick was hit, moved out of line for a little while, and later rejoined. Suddenly the British discovered that they were no longer closing the range. The Italians had turned away and were heading at their utmost speed for their base at Cagliari in the south of Sardinia. The British cruisers were making hits and the Italians had had enough.

Again the lookouts reported aircraft. It was the Swordfish and with a deep anxiety they were counted back; four, five, six. Eleven had gone out. Then there was a second report of three more. And then, incredibly, unbelievably, two more straggling well astern. At 13:15 the surface action ended. Five cruisers had fought off the Italian fleet.

From *Sheffield's* bridge, *Ark Royal* was seen to disappear in a forest of splashes and through these splashes shot the red flicker of explosions. They were the explosions of her own guns firing back.

She came out of the forest unharmed, infuriated and aggressive and the Regia Aeronautica went home.

The convoy went on to Alexandria and *Sheffield* went back to Gibraltar having fired some 249 six inch shells in an hour.

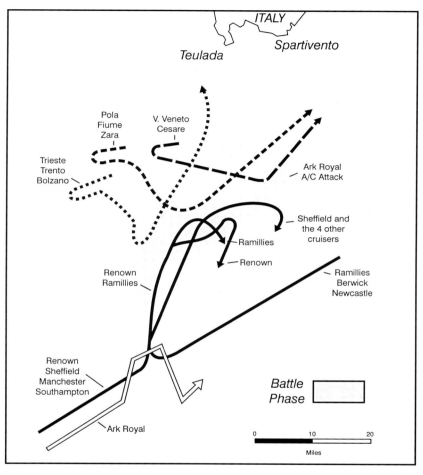

ITALY

Teulada　　Spartivento

Pola
Fiume
Zara

V. Veneto
Cesare

Trieste
Trento
Bolzano

Ark Royal
A/C Attack

Sheffield and
the 4 other
cruisers

Ramillies

Renown

Renown
Ramillies

Ramillies
Berwick
Newcastle

Renown
Sheffield
Manchester
Southampton

Battle
Phase

Ark Royal

0　　　　10　　　20

Miles

The Battle of Spartivento

Sink the Bismarck...
...not the Sheffield

Bismarck, May 1941

Well over half a century ago, Valentine's day 1939, Hitler launched what was probably the most capable battleship then built. Even as the new millennium approaches, the name *Bismarck* still draws reverence.

Having lost the First World War, Germany had been dis-armed which meant that in the 1930's Germany could re-equip its navy with the latest in warship design. *Bismarck* and her sister *Tirpitz* were the pride of some ten large warships built by the Nazis from the mid 1930's.

Sadly, most of Britain's battleships dated from the Great War with only *Hood*, *Repulse* and *Renown* being completed in the early 1920's. These three vessels being First World War designs.

Bismarck and *Tirpitz* posed a huge threat to Britain. Both ships were fast, being able to out-run all of Britain's battleships. Each was well armoured and armed with large 15 inch guns which could tear apart anything afloat. So, in short, *Bismarck* could out-run any British ship that could match her fire-power and completely out-gun any cruiser that could keep up with her.

In early 1941, when *Bismarck* was completed, the plan was that she should carry out 'commerce raiding', which entailed attacking convoys of supply ships that carried vital supplies of food, materials, aircraft and tanks from America, Britain's ally, to the United Kingdom. Already, German U-boats were causing havoc sinking hundreds of supply ships and the British situation was becoming critical. However, U-boats were slow and generally had to wait for convoys to come their way and, being relatively small, they carried only a dozen or so torpedoes. After these had been fired it normally led to a run home to re-load. *Bismarck,* in theory, could cruise the oceans at speed, knocking out the convoys at will.

In April 1941, Grand Admiral Raeder, the outstanding strategist of the Third Reich, was working on a plan to destroy Britain's convoys for good. Hitler expected that England would soon capitulate without these convoys. Raeder's plan was for a simultaneous breakout of German battleships from Baltic ports in the north and from Brest in western-occupied France. These ships would then rendezvous somewhere in the North Atlantic with the resulting battlegroup sinking convoy after convoy. In order to keep this battle group '*on station*' a fleet of five tankers and two supply ships were deployed around the Atlantic. Scout ships were also deployed to find convoys for the fleet. The operation was called '*Rheinubung*' or, in English, '*Operation Rhine*' and was planned for the second half of April, when the new moon would give dark nights for the breakout.

However, Raeder was to be unlucky. Of the four ships planned to take part, the battleship *Gneisenau* was torpedoed by a British aircraft; the heavy cruiser *Prinz Eugen* was slightly damaged by a magnetic mine and *Scharnhorst,* sister of the *Gneisenau,* was in refit which was taking longer to complete than planned.

Admiral Lütjens, complete with Iron Cross (Photo: Author's collection)

Finally, on May 18th 1941, under the command of Admiral Lütjens, *Bismarck* and the repaired *Prinz Eugen* left the Baltic port of Gdynia hoping to commence a surprise breakout. For three days all went well until an RAF photo-reconnaissance Spitfire which was on routine patrol taking pictures of the Norwegian coastline, when its pilot spotted large ships moving and took their photographs. Back in Britain, Naval Intelligence identified these ships as *Prinz Eugen* and *Bismarck* and, at once, Britain knew the suspected breakout had begun.

Admiral Sir John Tovey, in charge of the Home Fleet, dispatched the pride of the Royal Navy, the battle cruiser *Hood* and her squadron to attempt to locate the Germans. A day later *Bismarck* and *Prinz Eugen* could not be found anywhere near Norway. They must have headed out to sea, but to where?

Patrolling the Denmark Straights were two County Class cruisers, *Suffolk* and *Norfolk*. Just after 19:00 hours on the evening of the May 23rd, *Suffolk* sighted in the distance the silhouette of *Bismarck* with the similar, but smaller, profile of *Prinz Eugen* following. Captain Ellis of *Suffolk* immediately signalled to Admiral Holland in *Hood* informing him of *Bismarck's* position and course. Ellis then dived into the cover of a nearby mist bank knowing that engagement now would be futile. *Suffolk* had an early radar like *Sheffield's* so from the safety of the mist bank *Suffolk* and *Norfolk* could track the enemy.

Hood at Scapa Flow just before her loss (Photo: R.N.)

On *Hood,* Admiral Holland decided on a daring plan. He would intercept *Bismarck* and *Prinz Eugen* to the west of Iceland and, with the new but untested battleship *Prince of Wales,* they would attack *Bismarck.* At the same time, *Suffolk* and *Norfolk* would attack the smaller *Prinz Eugen* from behind.

At 05:30 on the morning of May 24th Admiral Holland spotted *Bismarck* and just before 06:00 both parties opened fire at a range of 25,000 yards and the battle commenced.

To the lay person this battle would appear to be well matched. The British, with a 45,000 ton battle cruiser accompanied by a brand new 35,000 ton battleship against the Germans with a 50,000 ton battleship and a 17,000 ton heavy cruiser.

However, with *Hood* being designed during the First World War for speed and firepower, she lacked deck armour. Battles of the First World War were fought at close range with shells fired at ships' sides. At long range, shells are fired at higher angles and tend to fall from a height on to the ships' decks. The Royal Navy knew that this was going to be a problem for *Hood.* Admiral Holland also knew this when he planned his attack on *Bismarck.* He was attacking more or less head on so that *Hood* and *Bismarck* would rapidly close on each other thus reducing battle time at long range. *Prince of Wales* had just been completed and had sailed complete with dockyard workers working to finish the ship.

Damage to Prince of Wales' funnel after her battle with Bismarck and Prinz Eugen. Prince of Wales was never considered lucky. This damage was caused when the ship was brand new. She went on to be finally sunk by Japanese aircraft off Malaya in December 1941 (Photo: R.N.)

Prinz Eugen hit *Hood* first starting fires that aided *Bismarck's* gunners fixing on *Hood.* The next salvo from *Bismark* blew *Hood* apart. The middle third of her just disappeared in smoke and flame. *Prince of Wales* following *Hood* swerved to miss the blazing wreckage and steered into a barrage of shells from *Bismarck* and *Prinz Eugen,* receiving seven hits. But, with her new guns jamming, her Captain John Leach decided enough was enough, did a U-turn around the sinking *Hood,* made smoke and a tactical withdrawal.

Hood, broken in two, sank in three minutes taking all but three of her 1,500 crew with her. Captain Ernst Lindeman of *Bismarck* wanted to pursue *Prince of Wales.* She would be an easy kill but, to his annoyance, Admiral Lütjens refused him. Their job was, after all, commerce raiding and orders from above were that units of the Royal Navy were to be avoided if possible.

There was also bad news for Lütjens. One of *Prince of Wales'* shells had hit *Bismarck* forward causing thousands of tons of water to flood the bow area and cutting off the forward fuel tanks. Maybe it would be a good idea to head for Brest for repairs.

Meanwhile, the crew of *Sheffield* had been enjoying the sun at Gibraltar when Force H was summoned to assist in the hunt for *Bismarck.* Her crew remained calm at this instruction. *Bismarck* was over 1,500 miles away and they thought that it would all be over before *Sheffield* got there, However, the Navy appeared to be throwing in everything. *Bismarck* was missing. A clever turn, whilst the following *Suffolk, Norfolk* and the damaged *Prince of Wales* zig-zagged, had let *Prinz Eugen* escape to hunt on her own and *Bismarck* break free from her pursuers.

It was thirty desperate hours before an RAF Catalina flying boat spotted *Bismarck* some seven hundred miles away from the safety of Brest. By this time Force H and *Sheffield* were a mere one hundred miles away.

Vice Admiral Somerville, commander of Force H, ordered *Sheffield* to head off to locate and shadow *Bismarck. Sheffield's* radar would have been vital, but considering the recent events, *Sheffield* was ordered to keep her distance.

At 18:00 on May 26th *Sheffield* located *Bismarck,* the first British vessel to make contact in forty hours. Meanwhile the aircraft carrier *Ark Royal* had sent fifteen Swordfish torpedo bombers to try and stop *Bismarck.* No-one on the *Ark* had noticed *Old Shiny* heading off. The orders given to the Swordfish crews were to set off and the first ship they would come across would be *Bismarck.*

The Swordfish crews soon found a radar contact, dived and attacked. In the poor weather and excitement of it all, few of the young crews wondered why

A Swordfish aircraft being loaded with a torpedo (Photo: R.N.)

Bismarck didn't fire on them or why she suddenly had two funnels. Eleven torpedoes were dropped before they realized their target was, in fact, *Old Shiny* and not a German battleship! Luckily most of the torpedoes exploded on contact with the sea with their new magnetic firing pistols being incorrectly set. Captain Larcom on *Sheffield's* bridge calmly dodged the last few torpedoes, assisted by the fact that *Sheffield* was now doing over 38 knots, eight knots faster than her designed speed!

As the aircraft turned to return to *Ark Royal* one of them was observed to signal "Sorry for the kippers", kipper being the nickname for a torpedo. Back on his flagship, *Renown,* Admiral Somerville was livid. In the failing light and in force six storm conditions he wondered if there would be time for his Swordfish aircraft to return and attack *Bismarck* as originally intended. If they couldn't slow *Bismarck* then, within hours, she would be in the safety of Brest and the battleships *Rodney* and *King George V* would not be able to catch up.

At 20:30 the second attack of Swordfish aircraft left *Ark Royal.* This time they were ordered to locate *Sheffield* first and then *Sheffield* would direct them to *Bismarck.* Fifteen aircraft attacked but eleven missed *Bismarck.* Two failed to drop their torpedoes and two scored hits. Of the two hits, one was midships and caused very little damage. However, the second exploded at the stern of *Bismarck* whilst her rudders were hard to port. The explosion wrecked *Bismarck's* steering machinery, thus her two rudders were jammed on full lock, the ship now unable to alter course.

Returning from the attack, two Swordfish flew low over *Sheffield,* their crews giving the thumbs up sign whilst one signalled 'hit'. *Old Shiny's* crew took off their caps and gave an almighty cheer! Suddenly, some of the crew saw the flashes of *Bismarck's* main 15 inch guns firing. They thought *Bismarck* must be firing at the Swordfish, but shell splashes a couple of miles away indicated that *Sheffield* was now the target. With her rudders jammed, *Bismarck* was sailing in circles and for a time was now head to head with *Sheffield.*

Bismarck engaged *Sheffield,* not because she wanted to, but because *Old Shiny* had sailed into her gun sights. *Bismarck* fired a few more salvos which fell yards from *Sheffield* filling the air with a mass of splinters and shell fragments.

Sheffield turned hard, increased speed and made smoke to hide her profile from *Bismarck's* gunners. By 21:45 it was all over. *Bismarck* had fired six salvos of 15 inch shells. None had hit *Old Shiny,* but near misses had caused splinter damage and fourteen casualties, of which three were later to die of their injuries. *Sheffield* was now joined by five destroyers, including the famous *Cossack.* Overnight they took over the shadowing of *Bismarck* as they waited for the big guns of *Rodney* and *KGV (King George V)* to arrive. During the darkness of night they fired their torpedoes at *Bismarck,* but to no avail.

Making smoke to hinder Bismarck's gunners. Smoke canisters are lit on Sheffield's stern (Photo: J.Cordy)

Splinter damage to Sheffield's after gun director (Photo: R.N.)

The after mast was almost sheared off
(Photo: J.Cordy)

To the disappointment of *Old Shiny's* crew, as the British battleships arrived, she and Force H were ordered away. Perhaps it was for units of the Home Fleet to avenge the loss of their flagship *Hood*.

It took the two Royal Navy battleships two hours to reduce the might of *Bismarck* to a blazing hulk. By 10:40 in the morning of May 27th 1941, *Bismarck* slid beneath the waves, 600 miles west of Brest with all but a hundred of her 2,000 crew. In the final battle *Bismarck* had scored no hits on British ships. The heavy cruiser *Dorsetshire* was credited with firing the salvo of torpedoes that sank *Bismarck*.

Damage to the wardroom which was luckily empty at the time *(Photo: R.N.)*

It is believed that towards the end, *Bismarck's* crew set off explosive charges in her engine room to assist her sinking.

As *Bismarck* sank, *Sheffield* and Force H headed back home to Gibraltar. They had expected the German air force to attack from French airfields but, in the event, only a few aircraft dared out.

Tragedy struck one last time for *Sheffield*. On May 29th one of her Walrus aircraft that had been sent on an anti-submarine patrol flew low past Force H's flagship, *Renown*. Unfortunately, it clipped part of *Renown's* superstructure and crashed into the sea with the death of five people.

Sheffield and Force H arrived at Gibraltar in the early evening to be welcomed by cheering crowds. *Old Shiny's* most famous action was over.

Two of Sheffield's dead are buried at sea, May 27th 1941 (Photo: R.N.)

Back at Gibraltar, Vice Admiral Somerville addresses Sheffield's crew (Photo: H.M.S.S.A)

Vice Admiral Somerville sent the following signal to *Sheffield:*

> **"Much regret to hear of your casualties whilst shadowing Bismarck.**
> **I wish to express my sympathy at the loss of your shipmates.**
> **I trust the wounded are progressing favourably."**

> **"I consider your tenacity and your shadowing was in a large degree**
> **responsible for the striking force and destroyers which fixed the Bismarck**
> **and led to her eventual destruction."**

In 1989 Dr. Robert Ballard, the ocean explorer who, in 1985, discovered the *Titanic,* went in search of *Bismarck.* He found her after a few weeks searching at a depth of three miles, upright in one piece and still looking as menacing as she did fifty years earlier.

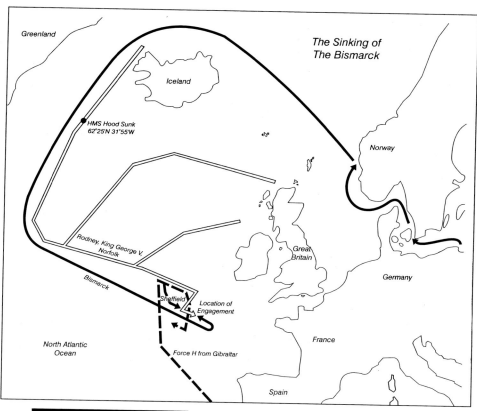

The Sinking of
The Bismarck

Greenland

Iceland

HMS Hood Sunk
62°25'N 31°55'W

Norway

Rodney, King George V,
Norfolk

Bismarck

Great
Britain

Germany

Sheffield

Location of
Engagement

France

North Atlantic
Ocean

Force H from Gibraltar

Spain

Jim Cordy, sailor on Sheffield during the
Bismark action.

"When Bismarck opened fire on us we
just sat tight and prayed that we were
not going to be another Hood"
(Photo: J. Cordy)

Captain Larcom on Sheffield's bridge. His cool-mannered reactions no doubt saved Old Shiny from damage during the Swordfish attack (Photo: H.M.S.S.A)

The Sinking of the Friedrich Breme

By June 8th 1941 *Sheffield* was on patrol again in the Atlantic. Seven days later *Old Shiny* came upon an unidentified merchant ship. A request was made for identification and the response came that the merchant ship was Panamanian bound for the UK. Captain Larcom didn't believe this. The merchant vessel wasn't slowing and so he ordered the ship to stop.

Suddenly, the merchant ship turned towards *Sheffield.* She appeared to be low in the water and, in fact, lifeboats could be seen being lowered. This merchant ship was the new German supply ship *Friedrich Breme* which was intended to supply the *Bismarck* and U-boats. To avoid capture her crew had scuttled her.

Once the lifeboats were away *Sheffield* opened fire. Rapidly the 15,000 ton ship caught fire, rolled over and sank.

Friedrich Breme on fire after receiving seventeen direct hits from Sheffield
(Photo: J.Cordy)

Ninety crewmen were rescued by *Sheffield,* twelve were injured of which two died. The dead were buried from the hangar deck with full military honours in front of their German crew mates.

Friedrich Breme's captain comes aboard Old Shiny. He claimed that he had served in the German Navy during the First World War and this was the second occasion that he had been a British prisoner of war
(Photos: J.Cordy)

Lifeboat from Friedrich Breme comes alongside

With full military honours, two German sailors are buried at sea from Sheffield's Hangar Deck. Both British and Germans were present

Edinburgh, Sheffield and Kenya during Operation 'Halberd'. Edinburgh was sunk in 1942 on Russian Convoy duty. She was carrying a cargo of gold that was recovered in 1982 (Photo: H.M.S.S.A)

At Rosyth, Scotland the prisoners were off-loaded and it was time for *Sheffield* to be dry-docked allowing maintenance on her hull.

A new Captain, Arthur Clarke took command in August 1941 and headed back to Gibraltar. *Old Shiny* was to join her half-sister *Edinburgh* and the cruiser *Kenya* to support a convoy bound for Malta. They joined the battleships *Rodney* and *Prince of Wales* and other cruisers and destroyers in a vast force that would be needed to get the convoy through if the Italian fleet took to sea.

As the fleet sailed east the weather was perfect. *Sheffield* was ahead of the convoy screening for enemy submarines. For two days all was quiet, but by September 27th the Force would pass Cape Bon, within range of the Italian Air Force. The first attack came at 13:00 from twelve Italian torpedo bombers. However *Ark Royal's* aircraft attacked and only six managed to drop their torpedoes, of which not one found its target. An hour later another attack came, but, with heavy fire coming from British ships, the Italians dropped their torpedoes too far away from their targets and again scored no hits.

A third attack was also beaten, but *Rodney, Prince of Wales, Sheffield* and *Edinburgh* were detached north-east where an enemy battle force had been reported some fifty miles away. *Ark Royal's* Swordfish torpedo bombers flew to locate the Italians, but by 17:00 nothing was found. The Italians had vanished. The evening was clear, perfect for enemy attacks, but difficult for British anti-aircraft gunners to see their targets. One merchant ship was torpedoed and lost.

The end of an Italian Aircraft (Photo: J.Cordy)

The convoy reached Malta the next day. RAF aircraft flew to meet the incoming fleet and as members of convoy 'Halberd' docked they were cheered by thankful Maltese as the Royal Marine band played.

Old Shiny's crew was looking forward to a run ashore at Malta, but it was not to be. Six hours after the convoy had successfully reached Malta *Sheffield* was off to Gibraltar again.

From Gibraltar it was back north to the cold of Arctic patrols and ceaseless storms.

Mine! A Night of Fear
on Old Shiny

In the late afternoon of March 4th 1942, *HMS Sheffield* disengaged from the lonely tanker at the head of snowbound Icelandic Seidisfiord. She turned seawards to start on her passage to rendezvous with the Home Fleet and other forces east of Jan Mayen Island. A further Russian convoy run was developing.

No-one on board looked forward to it. The barometer was falling fast, the sun set ominously, the wind was already blowing sharply from the north and it was clearly going to be a struggle against heavy seas to make the rendezvous on time. This chapter is taken from an eye witness account.

After a short exchange of messages with the patrolling trawler at the fjord's entrance the cruiser turned north up the ten mile lane between Iceland's coastline and the deep anti-submarine minefield to the east. The weather continued to deteriorate rapidly and at 21:00 the ship went to her nightly action stations for a final check through of communications before reverting to, what was euphemistically called, 'Night Action Rest'. She was already pitching heavily and down to a 14 knot speed. At the same time she was by then some ten miles clear of the northern edge of the minefield and a few minutes later at 21:15 the helm was put over to turn north-east for the night.

A few moments later, with the cruiser still swinging slowly to her new course, she gave a convulsive shudder, accompanied in a split second by a dull thud somewhere aft of the bridge, followed by a feeling as if she had been grasped by a giant hand, held in check for a moment and given a huge push forward. 'Torpedoed, and somewhere aft' was the immediate conclusion of everyone on the bridge.

Captain Clarke had long since decided that, where conditions at all allowed, he would in such circumstances stop his ship at once. He knew from others' experience that nothing more quickly and disastrously increased damage than the inrush of the sea against already weakened bulkheads abaft an open side. "Stop both engines, wheel amidships." Someone rang the alarm bells and all on the bridge turned to stare into the darkness astern.

As the noise of the engines died away the sound of running men could be heard. Fighting stations were, fortuitously, already manned, but now the damage control, repair and first-aid parties were assembling, all remaining watertight doors being closed, emergency action power supplies coming into operation and generally the ship's whole organisation rising to a first degree of readiness.

Beyond this the Captain felt disinclined to do more than wait. He trusted that a report of the damage would be relayed at the earliest possible moment. He equally knew that he had, at best, perhaps twenty minutes to do something if the ship was not to remain a sitting target for a determined submarine on the assumption, and he crossed his fingers, that the enemy had fired a full salvo of torpedoes in the first attack.

As it happened, the Commander and the Shipwright Officer were standing together near the mainmast at the moment of the explosion. The shock nearly knocked them both off their feet. The Shipwright started searching forward whilst the Commander slid down the ladder to the quarterdeck to work aft. He didn't have far to go. Abreast the after turret he could just see that beyond it the deck was torn and turned upwards and the heavy, disturbing surge of water below could be heard each time the ship, already abeam of the sea, rolled violently to port. Bracing himself against a railing he peered over the port side dimly to discern twisted plates abaft the armoured belt and a vast hole below disappearing into the darkness.

A closer inspection was imperative. A shout recalled the shipwright and together they cautiously made their way aft from the wardroom between decks to the heart of the damage. The watertight door opened fairly easily and they faced desolation. Huddled in a corner lay the Marine keyboard sentry, R. Wint, unconscious with severe head injuries. The port side of the hull was blown in with the main deck open to the sea as far as the centre-line. It was apparent that the hull had gone from just below the upper deck level to dangerously near the keel. However, it gave them some comfort in that it did seem that laterally the damage, though extending some forty feet, had stopped short of the watertight cross bulkheads both behind and before the centre of the hole.

All this had taken less time than it seemed to those on the bridge. The Captain assumed an air of patience which he was far from feeling. Though the Asdic operator had reported no contacts about, the urgent need to get under way, if this was at all possible, dominated his mind. Then the engine room telephoned up to say that all four shafts turned freely, though the Chief reserved his opinion about the state of the propellers. Immediately afterwards the Commander appeared on the bridge to tell of what he had found.

This was reasonably assuring, but given with the warning that the longitudinal strengths of the back end of the ship had obviously been greatly weakened, maybe by as much as a third. The tail which supported both inner shafts and, still more vital, the rudder, ought not to be subjected to further strain. With a word with the engine room to disconnect and tract the two inner shafts and with a sigh of hopefulness the Captain ordered "slow ahead both", precisely seventeen minutes after the explosion.

The vast hole in Sheffield's side (Photo: H.M.S.S.A)

Meantime, the Commander, also reported that the action damage repair parties were already on the job. A telephone line was being run over the quarterdeck to the steering compartment and temporary power and light supplies were in hand. The shipwrights were about to install a cement box to seal off water seeping through the join with the ship's side in the steering compartment and build a cofferdam over the same compartment's main deck hatch.

Finally, it was clear that whatever had happened it was from an external explosion so the Captain decided to break wireless silence. Things might get worse due to the gale evidently increasing in violence, and also in order that all should know that his ship was certainly no longer able to take part in the impending operation.

The Admiralty ordered two destroyers to assist *Sheffield* and also sent tugs from the Clyde just in case *Old Shiny* was too badly damaged to return home under her own steam.

Two destroyers, driven remorselessly through the filthy weather, reached *Sheffield* before midnight and they received the lasting thanks of everyone in the cruiser that they had been sent to assist.

Although thoughts of having to swim for it had been resolutely put aside, no-one found it pleasant to crawl along at five knots in the open ocean with the feeling that there might he a submarine about, waiting for dawn to see what more could be done.

The two escorts adopted a circular patrol around their charge and kept it up hour after hour. The discomfort in the heavy weather can be understood with one leg pitching into it, the next one rolling heavily, the third corkscrewing before a following sea and the fourth rolling again. However uncomfortable things were on the bigger ship, there was at least none of the ever changing violence suffered in the destroyers, robbing everybody of any possibility of satisfying rest.

The night wore on and, though the wind had risen to gale force, the sea was seemingly not much worse. The first glimmering of daylight gave a comforting sight of the snow covered coastline and *Sheffield* had almost reached safety. Radio silence was again broken to report that no further damage had developed and anticipated a safe arrival at Seidisfiord before noon. The tugs were recalled to the Clyde.

Nearing the entrance, the destroyers were detached to fuel in turn whilst the other established an anti-submarine patrol to seaward and the cruiser turned thankfully into the relative tranquillity of the fjord.

There were two problems to resolve: how to make the ship sufficiently seaworthy for the onward passage of seven hundred miles to Scapa Flow, and then to a repair yard and, while doing so, how she might be protected whilst lying in a fjord which had nothing in the way of defence.

Apart from the obvious necessity of a permanent offshore anti-submarine patrol to seaward, the cruiser established an observation post at the entrance. Her main armament being controlled by portable wireless equipment in the event that an attack by an enterprising surface warship came about. In addition, the cruiser's Walrus aircraft were daily flown to the limit of their engines' endurance on seaward reconnaissance.

One of Sheffield's Walrus flying boats on the catapult ready for take off. By the end of the eighty foot catapult the aircraft would be moving at eighty miles an hour. During temporary mine repairs at Iceland, Old Shiny's two Walrus were kept busy patrolling for German U-boats (Photo: R.N.)

Meanwhile, the more serious issue of what to do for the best about the damage was discussed with a salvage officer who appeared on the scene with startling rapidity. It was clearly beyond local resources to make the ship watertight, but essentially the need was to prevent any further battering of the after cross bulkhead.

It was decided to construct a semi-flexible screen of timbers over the 800 sq. ft. hole, rather like a Venetian blind, holding it in place by wires wrapped right around the after part of the ship and braced into the hull shape by further wires to the upper deck.

On the first days of these preliminary discussions and mustering of gear, one other duty fell to the ship: the laying to rest of the remains of the dead Marine sentry in the little cemetery beyond the nearby village. This was done with full naval honours and the local fisherfolk watched the passing with kindly and sympathetic reverence.

As the subsequent days wore on, the shield took shape. The resident Naval Officer of the district aided and abetted the stripping of a nearby pier, which everyone hopefully assumed was derelict, of its heavy timbers. Every wire the ship possessed was sought out.

After a lot of hard work in high winds and snowstorms by shipwrights, divers and artificers, the final bracing was completed eleven days later and the ship sailed for a trial run.

This revealed at once that the port inner propeller shaft was not going to stand the strain. A further week of work ensued, exhausting the last resources of ship and shore before a further trial suggested that with fine weather there was reasonable hope of keeping the whole intact.

With forecasts giving a fair assurance of nothing worse than a mild swell, and with an escort of three frigates, the ship set forth. During the last night of the three days passage parts of the shield gave ominous evidence of breaking up. However, the cruiser ultimately steamed triumphantly through the gates of Scapa Flow and into the hands of the Fleet Repair Ship.

In parting with her escort a pleasant incident occurred. The Lt. Commander of the senior frigate hoisted the well-known two-flag signal 'Manoeuvre well executed'. This signal is normally reserved for use by a senior officer to convey his appreciation of a junior's actions, but its brevity and exceptional employment by a junior on this occasion warmed the heart of all on board *Old Shiny.* The approbation of a brother seaman is a treasure beyond price.

There was not much of consequence to be done at Scapa Flow. Bright lights beckoned to a ship's company which had not seen civilization for nine months. Three days later she sailed again for the Tyne and after an eventful run down the east coast swept channel, the lady spread her weatherbeaten skirts and

Looking astern, a mass a cables hold the wooden shield in place (Photo: J.Dean)

settled gracefully on to the blocks in the dry dock to expose the full extent of her wound.

Among the visitors came Admiralty experts who examined, measured, photographed, calculated and arrived at the unanimous conclusion that the damage had been caused by a floating mine into which the ship had swung on her turn. Almost certainly it had been a British one from the nearby Northern minefield. Mines that break away should render themselves innocuous, but if trailing an extensive mooring, the safety mechanism may not always work.

So that was that. The ship's company took rather a poor view of this conclusion, but was later heartened by a story in which Lord Haw Haw had come up with a claim that a large English warship had been destroyed off Iceland. This suggested that the spate of wireless traffic had conveyed a crisis of some kind to the enemy's naval authorities, who decided to cash in with a bit of propaganda, even though it was guesswork at best.

Sheffield felt, however, that the last laugh was hers. She had come through one of the most testing experiences with flying colours.

Mutiny

It took three months for the workmen of Palmer's yard to repair *Old Shiny*. The Navy was far from impressed with the yard: the unions repeatedly called the workers out for more pay; anything moveable went missing and the management of the yard failed to inform the Navy that all dockyard workers were going on annual leave before work on the *Sheffield* was due to be finished, leaving the ship's crew to complete the work.

The opportunity had then been taken to update *Sheffield's* radar and improve her anti-aircraft arrangement. Early in July *Old Shiny* was out of dry dock, but she had only been out for a few days when, one evening, a supply ship rammed her forward and slid down the cruiser's side damaging all the new paint work. Luckily the damage was only superficial, but it did mean that *Sheffield's* crew got an extra week in Newcastle whilst repairs were carried out.

On July 20th *Sheffield* left the Tyne for Scapa Flow to spend a few weeks

Sheffield off Iceland 1941 (Photo: H.M.S.S.A)

'working up' her crew and getting everything ship shape. A third of *Old Shiny's* crew was new and this was, in effect, a new commission. En route a lookout spotted a mine off the starboard bow. Not another mine so soon! *Sheffield* engaged with her close range guns, but to no effect. Perhaps 'Jerry' was laying wooden mines to waste British ammunition!

Sheffield eventually gave up, leaving the mine for the mine sweepers. Four weeks of training were carried out at Scapa Flow, getting the ship ready for combat. The guns were fired, torpedoes launched and, to familiarise the crew with damage, the ship would be heeled over to maximum list, lights turned out and the crew expected to carry out their normal duties. From time to time orders would suddenly change. Crew would be ordered to launch boats, row around the ship and then recover the boats, all in the name of shaping up the young crew. For target practice a rock off the Scottish coast, Shag Skerry, would be used. *Sheffield* would often practise close to the rock with the large battleships up to fourteen miles away. Sailors could find the firing confusing. They would see the flash of the battleship's distant guns then the flash of the shells exploding on Shag Skerry followed by the explosion from the rock then hear the sound of the big guns firing!

All ready for service by September 4th, *Sheffield* arrived at Glasgow on the 7th with her crew allowed a night on the town. The following day *Old Shiny* moored down the Clyde at an anchorage known as 'The Tail of the Bonk'. An hour later, some rather odd supplies started to arrive: husky dogs, sledges, skis, drums of paraffin, anti-aircraft guns and a motor launch were all loaded into the hangars whilst a strange mix of civilians, Norwegians and soldiers also embarked, but where for and why? Later Captain Clarke came over the tannoy and told the crew that they were off to Hvalfiord, the fleet's base in Iceland. Hvalfiord was where convoys for Russia would meet with elements coming from the United States and the United Kingdom. In company with the heavy cruiser *Cumberland, Sheffield* arrived at Hvalfiord on September 10th to join the other heavy cruisers *Norfolk, Suffolk* and *London*. Hvalfiord made an ideal base for the warships and the convoys. It was a vast harbour formed by a natural fjord surrounded by high mountains making it difficult to attack from the air.

Four days later the fleet set sail. The convoy known as CG18 was under the command of Admiral Bonham Carter in the *Norfolk,* the destination Russia. *Sheffield* was to be part of a shadowing group north of the convoy that would come to assist if the convoy should be attacked. It was then that the mystery of strange cargo was resolved. A month or so earlier the battleship *Tirpitz*, sister to the *Bismarck,* had, with several other German ships, raided the island of

Hvalfiord, Iceland. The high mountains provided an ideal base for the Royal Navy in the war
(Photo: J.Dean)

Spitzbergen where the Norwegians had maintained a weather station supplying the allies with all year round weather reports. The Germans had bombarded the island, landed troops and wrecked everything they could. However, the Norwegians had managed to escape inland. *Sheffield's* job was to assist in re-supplying the weather station before winter set in. It was understood that the Germans retained a close eye on Spitzbergen anticipating the allies returning. Therefore Admiral Bonham Carter wanted the re-supplying operation to be carried out as quickly as possible. At 14:00 in the afternoon of the 18th, *Sheffield,* anchored off Barentsberg, Spitzbergen. With no jetty *Old Shiny's* shipwrights had made a raft of planks to carry her cargo, including guns, ashore. They off-loaded enough supplies to keep the Norwegians going through the winter months. With the coming of winter, the Germans would not be able to attack again through the pack-ice.

Sheffield left Barentsberg at 21:00 and headed south. The way south was uneventful, but the sea was covered with ice flows. On one of these flows sat three polar bears quite happily, despite the fact that they were many miles out to sea. Sometimes these bears could reach Iceland, much to the concern of the Icelandics!

Sheffield returned to Scapa Flow, rested for two weeks and then headed for Northern Ireland, docking in Belfast Lough. To the great disappointment of *Old Shiny's* crew, no leave was granted. However, the next day, to their great surprise, a total of six hundred American soldiers suddenly arrived on board.

They were National Guard troops fresh from America. *Sheffield's* crew quizzed them about what was happening, but they knew nothing either. As evening arrived *Sheffield* set sail south towards the Atlantic where she was to join a vast convoy of vessels, including famous liners, *Monarch of Bermuda* and *Ile de France* (used in the 60's film 'The Last Voyage')

Operation Torch, convoy at sea (Photo: H.M.S.S.A)

After seven days at sea an amateur navigator on board thought that the convoy was approaching the Caribbean but, on the eighth day, they were told that the vast convoy was carrying a whole army to invade North Africa in 'Operation Torch'. *Sheffield's* American guests seemed happy to finally know of their destination. However, they were not used to life on board ship, with a few still wearing their life jackets since leaving Belfast!

As the invasion fleet approached the Mediterranean, *Sheffield* was detached to Gibraltar. Arriving in Gib' great care had to be taken. It was known that the area of Spain that surrounded Gibraltar was full of German spies. It would throw the surprise of the intended landing if these spies saw *Old Shiny* full to her seams

The Americans leave Sheffield on their way to land at Algiers (Photo: J.Dean)

with American G.I's. Orders were therefore given that any American wanting to go on deck must wear a Royal Navy uniform.

Sheffield berthed against the battleship *Nelson*. What a sight that must have been for *Nelson's* crew: *Sheffield*, with hundreds of crew on deck, smoking cigars dressed in Navy bell bottoms but with G.I. tops. *Nelson's* crew must have thought *Sheffield's* crew had all gone 'bomb happy!'

Come evening *Old Shiny* set sail for Algiers. *Sheffield's* job was to take her Americans to the land and force entry at the harbour. A small commando force would then try to capture the Vichy French Naval Commander, Admiral Darlen. *Sheffield's* 6- inch guns would provide back-up if required.

Two old British destroyers *Broke* and *Malcolm*, stripped of their guns, came alongside *Sheffield* to take the Americans to their destination. *Old Shiny* would stay off-shore. The French were ready and as soon as the old ships approached the harbour shells were poured in on them. From the distance the men of *Sheffield* couldn't see what was going on. *Malcolm* returned back rather worse for wear and *Broke* had been sunk, with the French Foreign Legion capturing the Americans. Admiral Darlen was not to be found.

Tragedy was to strike *Sheffield* herself that day. Whilst heading away from Algiers there was a sudden bang from the starboard side. A small naval vessel *HMS Cadmus*, a mine sweeper, had collided with *Sheffield*. Fortunately, the

Landings at Algiers. Two old destroyers head off into the distance (Photo: H.M.S.S.A)

impact had been a glancing blow down the cruiser's side, but a young sailor was missing. He was later found dead entangled in the plane's catapult. He'd been taking a break on deck when the collision occurred and was caught in the impact. He was buried at sea the following day.

Sheffield was then sent to sort out the coastal French Foreign Legion that were giving the allies some trouble. However, with one sight of *Sheffield* and her 6-inch guns, they gave up without a fight.

The Vichy French may have given in, but the German and Italian air forces had not. Air attack warnings came as *Sheffield's* radar had spotted incoming aircraft. *Old Shiny* went to full speed, closed water tight doors and port holes and went to action stations. First came the Italians. Flying high they dropped their bombs high and although their near misses shook *Old Shiny,* no damage was caused. Next came the Germans with their Stuka dive bombers. They attacked from the sun, unaware that *Sheffield's* radar had already seen them. There were three more attacks but no hits. It must be remembered that when *Old Shiny* was at action stations most of her crew would be sealed up in gun turrets, engine rooms, shell handling rooms, etc, unable to see the incoming attacks. They were deafened, not by the noise of the incoming aircraft, but by the deafening roar of *Sheffield's* anti-aircraft guns firing thousands of rounds of shells a minute. The fear, apprehension and terror of the young crew must have been something else.

Cadmus the minesweeper which collided with Sheffield

Once the attacks were over it was discovered that one of the seamen's mess decks was riddled with holes, not from enemy action, but from a stray anti-aircraft shell from another British ship exploding near *Sheffield's* bow. Seventeen men on deck had been wounded.

It was November 9th, a day remembered by *Old Shiny's* crew for the air attacks. At 17:30, with dusk approaching, another attack was spotted by the crew on radar. The enemy thought they had the surprise of failing light, but the radar operator shouted "Planes coming East Red 90" and then the enemy came in for a shock. Maybe carrots did work! *Sheffield* zig-zagged to avoid torpedoes, the poor gunmen just relying on radar bearings for target firing into pitch black. These were the days before radar-guided guns or missiles.

As aircraft dropped the torpedoes and flew over *Old Shiny* some over-enthusiastic gunners turned around their guns and fired at the enemies back. This soon stopped, however, after words from the Petty Officer "I don't want you silly b......s wasting ammunition on aircraft that have dropped their torpedoes. It's the next one that has not that may get you!"

For what must have seemed a lifetime the attacks continued, in fact for just one hour. Luckily *Sheffield* was unharmed. Some merchant ships had been hit and some planes downed. With some Italian crew being picked up it seemed that the stories of the Italians' fighting ability didn't apply to their pilots.

Noon the following day, Stuka dive bombers came. They dived on to their target producing an awful scream designed to scare the enemy. Then came more Italian torpedo bombers. Crewman John Dean had a brilliant idea. The gunners were having terrible problems seeing attacking aircraft. They

CERTIFICATE FOR WOUNDS AND HURTS

These are to Certify the Right Honourable the Lords Commissioners of the Admiralty that

(Name in full)   (Rank or Rating)   (Official Number)

James McMinnis   Ordinary Seaman   C/JX.352049

belonging to His Majesty's Ship SHEFFIELD

was wounded on 8th November 1942 as shown on

the reverse hereof:

and that I ~~have~~ having enquired into the circumstances

in which he received the wound stated, and ~~having~~

~~heard the evidence of~~

(Insert Name and Rank or Rating)

~~who certified the sentence, considered that he was then~~

actually On His Majesty's Service in acting

as lookout in the Air Defence Position when he was struck by

shell splinters during an engagement with Italian aircraft.

Injured or Wounded

Injury or Wound

Here describe the manner in which the injury was received and also the particular act of duty or form of physical recreation in which it was incurred as required by Article 1419 of the King's Regulations.

Delete when case is investigated by Captain.

~~Signatures and Ranks of Investigating Officers~~

Signature of Officer or Man injured   *J. McMinnis*

Date 15th 19 42   Signature of Captain   *[signature]*

November   H.M.S. SHEFFIELD

NOTE:- The grant of a Hurt Certificate to a Petty Officer or Man is to be noted on his Service Certificate.

Injury certificate for James McMinnis

58

approached from the sun, the enemy knowing that the gunners would have difficulty in seeing them. So, John grabbed some welding goggles that he had in his locker and, whilst wearing them, he could see into the sun. John could then tell the gunners where to fire. That day *Sheffield* shot down two aircraft and luckily only had two near misses themselves.

Anti-aircraft fire from the 4 inch guns (Photo: H.M.S.S.A)

As the day ended they headed back to North Africa and Bougie Bay which had been attacked during daylight by the Luftwaffe. About twelve ships had been sunk. One of *Sheffield's* crew had been on board one of the sunk vessels. He had manned one of the machine guns during the attack and continued to fight despite the fact that the ship was sinking. Only when his position was awash did he stop. For this he was awarded the Distinguished Service Medal.

Two days of air attacks followed and then *Old Shiny* was ordered back to Scapa Flow. *Sheffield* would first escort some empty vessels from the African landings back to Gibraltar. *Old Shiny's* luck held. In the moonlight a crewman on deck saw what he thought were streaks in the sea caused by torpedoes. They were too fast for dolphins and were heading for *Sheffield*, but they ran astern by twenty feet. *Sheffield* went to full speed, a U-boat was thought to have been spotted earlier.

Back at Scapa, the crew were unhappy. With all the damage caused by the air attacks and the collision with *Cadmus* they thought that *Sheffield* would have docked for a few weeks giving them some leave. *Old Shiny* would have temporary repair at Scapa, but the Navy were short of ships such as *Sheffield*. In the previous year four of *Sheffield's* sisters had been sunk, one had been heavily damaged and *Belfast* had only just returned to service following two years repairs necessitated by mine damage.

In the morning, dockyard workers arrived with their equipment and commenced repair. The mood on *Sheffield* grew worse. They had been at sea for ages, had been subjected to air attacks for days and lived in constant dread of torpedoes or mines. Enough was enough. Their leave was overdue!

That night a knife was thrown at a Marine Sentry. Fortunately for him it was the handle that hit him. Also all the shipyard equipment was thrown overboard. No-one knew who the culprits were. Divers were sent down as morning broke, but they could not locate the missing equipment. Captain 'Nobby' Clarke was far from pleased. The men responsible could be tried for treason. Leave would be granted after their next trip. The crew were not impressed as the next trip was to Russia from where there might be no return. It was better to end up in the warm Mediterranean than the freezing North Atlantic, where a sailor would only last minutes in the water if *Old Shiny* was to be torpedoed. *Sheffield's* sister *Edinburgh* had gone that way.

That was it for *Old Shiny's* mutiny. The crew respected Captain Clarke and knew his position and that he was a man of his word. Similar incidents apparently occurred during World War Two on other war ships. Allegedly the whole affair was classified and crew members told that it was to be covered by the fifty year rule.

A week later repairs were completed and *Sheffield* escorted a convoy to Iceland where, as normal, they joined the American contingent of ships bound for Russia. There followed ten days of hell, not from the enemy, but from the weather. Spray from the bow turned to ice and hit any crew members above deck like bullets. Whilst above deck the crew had to be careful. If they took off their gloves their hands would stick to the railings ripping away layers of skin. Men would have to use steam hoses to keep gun turrets moving and prevent anti-aircraft guns from freezing. Ice is heavy and it became important that *Sheffield* didn't become top heavy with ice, or she might roll in the swell and perhaps continue to roll and turn turtle.

Above: Hazard to be on deck. Below: Not pleasant for the lookouts working in the elements (Photos: H.M.S.S

Ice covers Sheffield's boat davits
(Photo: H.M.S.S.A)

With a temperature of -40°, crew on deck would wear three pairs of socks, sea boots, pants, long johns, Arctic pants, trousers, vest, string vest, shirt, pullover, jacket, overcoat, Arctic coat, balaclava, Arctic cap, mittens and Arctic gloves.

Old Shiny anchored at Polyarnve, the Russian Naval base near Murmansk. With the temperature still 40° below, German air bases were just 20 minutes flying time away. Within two hours the Luftwaffe attacked, but again nothing hit *Sheffield*.

The following day tragedy struck *Jamaica,* a cruiser accompanying *Sheffield.* Three crew members were working on *Jamaica's* hull when they fell into the freezing sea. Despite being picked up within five minutes two were dead.

That night the Russians laid on some entertainment: their fleet choir and a team of dancers. Suddenly the crew remembered it was Christmas day and the Russians gave a few bottles of Vodka and turkeys were transferred from the *Jamaica.*

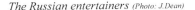

The Russian entertainers (Photo: J.Dean)

Clearing ice from the anchor chains in temperatures of -40°
(Photos: H.M.S.S.A)
Minesweeper J85 alongside Sheffield, anchored near Murmansk, Christmas 1941

December 1941, making Sheffield's vast Christmas pudding for her 800 or so crew
(Photos: J. McMinnis)

The North Atlantic's Worst Storm

So then it was off to Russia again, but as *Sheffield* was on passage to Iceland the barometer rapidly fell and the seas got rougher and rougher. Barometer readings fell to 960 millibars leading to high winds of 120 mph and seas like mountains, higher than *Old Shiny's* bridge. Spray blown off the waves by the winds made it almost impossible to distinguish the sea from the sky.

Uncomfortable view from the bridge (Photo: J.Dean)

In these conditions progress was impossible. The propellers were kept turning just to keep control of the rudder as, in such seas, the ship had to be maintained head-on otherwise she could roll over. Nautically this action is called 'heaving to'. Suddenly large explosions were heard astern. The depth charges carried on the quarter deck behind the rear 6-inch gun turret had been washed overboard, but had luckily exploded away from *Sheffield*.

Next a vast wave crashed down on 'A' turret, the forward 6-inch gun turret, with a force so large that it peeled a three ton section of the roof away. This section had been held in place by 120 one inch brass bolts. Several hundred tons of water flooded the turret causing some serious injuries to crew in the turret. Flood water drained down in to *Old Shiny's* innards with every successive wave adding more water. *Sheffield* was down by the bows and became sluggish. The 9,000 ton cruiser had a thousand tons of water in her bows and concern was mounting. No ships were near to help and privately the crew pondered on their survival.

Worse was still to come. The pounding of waves was caving in the deck on the bows. If the fore deck failed then *Sheffield* would be inundated with water within a minute and she would probably sink within five minutes.

Rapidly every spare man was shoring up the deck with wooden beams. The plan worked, the beams held, the water stayed out. *Sheffield* endured this storm for twelve hours before it subsided. Fifteen hours later food began to be served as it had been impossible to cook during the storm with the decks pitching in every direction.

Left: Waves crash down onto her bows. Right: Mountainous seas tower above her decks (Photos: James McMinni

Sheffield was a mess. Even sailors were sea-sick in these conditions. The decks were waterlogged, not only from the leaking sea water, but from waste flowing from the toilets as the ship rolled at crazy angles from bow to stern. She had been through one of the worst storms ever experienced in the North Atlantic with winds of up to 150 miles an hour and with a barometer reading that had fallen off the scale.

Left: The damaged forward 'A' turret

Right: Remains of one of the ship's wooden boats. Sheffield seemed to lose these boats during every storm she suffered (Photos: J.Dean)

The storm had blown *Sheffield* two hundred miles south and caused extreme damage. Not only had 'A' turret lost its roof but it was totally bent and unable to move on its mountings. All forward decks were damaged. Hence, *Sheffield* would need a few months repair and, in effect, an end to her commission.

72

Shelling the Italians and Sinking the Scharnhorst

By the end of February 1943 *Old Shiny* was docked at Dalmuir on the Clyde to start three months of repair. Apart from repairing storm damage the opportunity was taken to remove *Sheffield's* aircraft facilities. With the total adoption of radar and the introduction of the escort carriers, the little old seaplanes were of little use. In fact the recovery operation, requiring the ship to slow down and hoist up the Walrus aircraft, could expose the cruiser to U-boat attack.

By June *Sheffield* was ready, gleaming in her new paint, much of her crew being new to her. Thus *Sheffield* headed to Scapa Flow for a month of training culminating in a visit to Plymouth on July 22nd. Plymouth was, and still is, one of the Royal Navy's main bases. The other base, Portsmouth, was much larger than *Sheffield's* base of Chatham. Chatham was the base for cruisers, destroyers and frigates. The huge base of Plymouth Devonport was home to large battleships and aircraft carriers.

By late September it was time for *Old Shiny* to go into double figures and gain her tenth battle honour. The allied armies advancing up through Italy were facing stiff opposition from the Germans around Salerno. They had called upon the US and Royal Navy to bombard the enemy from the sea.

Sheffield steamed at full speed stopping at Gibraltar and Malta, commencing her own bombardment on September 28th. This job could be risky. The Germans had a new deadly weapon, the glider boat. Released high away from the guns of the target, the bomb would be radio controlled from the aircraft to the target. In effect this weapon was the great grandfather of the Exocet missile.

Already the First World War battleship *Warspite* had been hit and badly damaged, so had the cruiser *Uganda* and the American cruiser *Philadelphia*. Having embarked Army liaison officers *Sheffield* steamed around the area shelling as required by the army.

The bombardment of Salerno (Photo: H.M.S.S.A)

Come October 5th Naples had been taken. *Old Shiny* was low on ammunition and, with the situation easing, she headed for Malta. Malta was a strange sight. The surviving vessels of the Italian Navy which had surrendered had been ordered to Malta. At peace now, their war was over. The same ships that *Old Shiny* had engaged three years earlier during the battle of Spartivento were now prizes of the Allies and the Royal Navy. Home at Plymouth by November 20th, three days leave were granted. The last days of 1943 must surely be quiet.

Perhaps it was not to be. By December 7th *Sheffield* had joined her half-sister *Belfast* and the old heavy cruiser *Norfolk* in Scapa Flow. Yet another Russian convoy, code-named JW55B, was out-bound northward to Russia.

Based at Kola Inlet the cruiser would protect the merchant ships of the convoy as they entered the dangerous area of Barents Sea where *Sheffield* had earlier gained battle honours. The Navy expected the German battleship *Scharnhorst*, the last remaining enemy capital ship in fighting order, to come out and attack the convoy that was carrying vital supplies that Russia required to continue their fight against the Nazis.

Scharnhorst was an awesome opponent. Though smaller than *Bismarck*, she carried nine 11-inch guns, twelve 5.9-inch guns and fourteen 4.1-inch guns. Unlike much of the German Surface Fleet *Scharnhorst* had enjoyed a successful career. In 1940 she had sunk the armed liner *Rawalpindi* and the

The Scharnhorst (Photo: Author's collection)

aircraft carrier *Glorious* and survived countless British bombings whilst docked at Brest in France.

At sea *Sheffield, Belfast* and *Norfolk* had been at 'battle stations' since Christmas Eve. There were reports that enemy vessels had left their Norwegian base of Altenfiord. The weather was bad: snow showers, poor visibility, and extreme cold. By Boxing Day the three British cruisers were on intercept course with the Germans. To the west the battleship *Duke of York* and the cruiser *Jamaica* were attempting to get behind the enemy.

Scharnhorst was making for the convoy, her captain unaware of the presence of the British warships. That was until the 8-inch shells from *Norfolk* blew away the German ship's radar. Now *Scharnhorst* turned southward pursued by the British but, in heavy seas, the smaller cruiser couldn't keep up with *Scharnhorst*.

Admiral Burnett, who was in charge, decided that *Scharnhorst* would attempt to out-run the cruiser and then alter course to make a new attack on the convoy. So he turned his cruiser north-east towards the convoy. Burnett was correct. *Scharnhorst* circled eastward and then north-east. Two hours later the German was ten miles from the British.

Old Shiny opened fire first but *Scharnhorst* fired on *Norfolk* and gained some hits that started fires aft. *Sheffield* was straddled by shells but only suffered splinter damage. The Germans, however, had suffered seventeen minutes of hits. It was time to forget the convoy and go home.

Scharnhorst turned and headed home at full speed pursued for three hours by *Sheffield, Belfast* and the damaged *Norfolk*. Suddenly, however, disaster struck

Old Shiny. Intense vibration rocked her stern. A heavy bearing on one of the the propeller shafts had failed. The shaft would have to be locked and speed reduced. *Old Shiny* was out of the battle.

Belfast and *Norfolk* continued engaging the enemy at 18:30, now joined by the 14-inch guns of *Duke of York* and the cruiser *Jamaica*.

Scharnhorst received hit after hit, but her fast speed was saving her. Destroyers were despatched to torpedo the Germans. The four little destroyers *Savage, Saumarez, Scorpion* and *Stord* fired sixteen torpedoes, of which one hit one of *Scharnhorst's* boiler rooms reducing her speed.

Old Shiny was now making 22 knots but still too far away to join the fight. However, the enemy ship was now being pounded by one battleship and three cruisers. Four more British destroyers torpedoed *Scharnhorst*. Around fourteen torpedoes hit and, shortly before 22:00, a couple of massive explosions were heard. The ageing German fought to the end, rolled over and sank. From a crew of 2,000 only 36 survived. *Sheffield* arrived at the scene too late. All was over, but from *Scharnhorst's* watery grave eerie rumblings and explosions could be heard. The sea was a mass of oil and broken wreckage from the sinking battleship.

By tea time the next day, December 27th, *Sheffield, Belfast* and *Norfolk* were back at Kola Inlet and it was time for a delayed Christmas Day! *Sheffield* had gained her last battle honour of World War Two.

Old Shiny returned home to have her defective propeller shaft repaired at Birkenhead and by February 1944 repairs were complete. The Sheffield Star newspaper had donated 100,000 cigarettes to *Old Shiny*, a hundred for every man on board. How different things were years ago!

Until March *Sheffield* just exercised, but on March 30th it was time for action again in the form of 'Operation Tungsten'.

Bismarck's sister *Tirpitz* was moored at Altenfiord in Norway. *Tirpitz* posed the same threat to convoys as *Bismarck* had done in 1941. Considerable efforts had been spent trying to sink *Tirpitz*. The Royal Navy had attacked using mini submarines causing only moderate damage. Altenfiord provided a safe haven, well defended by anti-aircraft guns and anti-torpedeo nets. The *Tirpitz* would be a hard nut to crack.

Reports suggested that the *Tirpitz* might sail soon so the Navy were ordered to attack using aircraft. *Sheffield* sailed with the aircraft carriers *Victorious*, *Furious* and the escort carriers *Emperor*, *Pursuer*, *Searcher* and *Fencer* to a point 250 miles north of the target. *Old Shiny's* expert radar operators would keep an eagle-eye out for the Luftwaffe attacks sent from airfields in Norway.

On Monday April 3rd ten Barracuda aircraft took off, each carrying a single bomb and flew to their target. No German aircraft came up to fight. The Barracuda scored nine hits and the second wave scored even more. Two Barracudas were lost, one hundred sailors aboard *Tirpitz* were killed and repair would take six months. Lancasters of 9 and 617 squadrons, under RAF Bomber Command, would finish off *Tirpitz* a few months later with their Barnes Wallace designed 'Grand Slam' bombs, the largest conventional bomb ever made. These huge bombs were also manufactured in Sheffield and, even today, one is preserved in the Kelham Island Museum in Sheffield.

Sheffield's radar had seen nothing and all had been quiet. Back home in Scapa Flow little was happening. Much of the Royal Navy had gone east to fight the Japanese. German surface activity was now non-existent and the U-boats were being sunk by the dozen.

On D-Day, Tuesday June 6th 1944, *Sheffield* was still at Scapa. Her crew seemed shocked that they weren't involved. Indeed, the first they learned of the allied landing was from the BBC News. *Sheffield* was held in reserve in case the German Navy attacked the landing force. However, the Germans stayed at home.

There were German ships in Norway. *Old Shiny* was sent north to sniff them out, but again the enemy stayed indoors. By June 25th *Sheffield* turned for home and left the cold of the arctic for the final time.

The need for *Old Shiny* in European waters was decreasing, but the need for warships in the east against Japan was pressing, so *Sheffield* was to be prepared for such service. However, British shipyards were too busy so work would have to be carried out at South Boston Navy Yard, Boston, Massachusetts, USA.

Back at Chatham, *Sheffield's* home that she'd rarely visited during the war years, many of her crew left for other appointments. Much of the crew that would take *Old Shiny* to the United States were Canadian.

The veteran cruiser of twelve battles docked at Boston Navy Yard on July 25th. Almost at once the well organised American work force started work. *Sheffield*

Sheffield held in reserve at Scapa Flow on D-Day (Photo: James McMinnis)

was to lose one of her four 6-inch gun turrets, a turret mounted aft of the second funnel. In its place additional anti-aircraft guns would be fitted as now much of the threat was from the air. Of the twenty major Royal Navy warships sunk during World War Two only *Hood* and *Glorious* were lost due to surface action. *Courageous, Ark Royal, Barham, Royal Oak, Manchester, Edinburgh* and *Eagle* were lost to U-boats and the rest to air attack. The condition of *Old Shiny* was worse than expected and repair would take longer. In February 1945 a new Captain, J.Eaton, took over.

On May the 2nd *Sheffield* headed home. The war in Europe now over, *Old Shiny's* refit would be completed in the UK. With her sailed thirty British boys who, earlier in the war, had been evacuated to the US, complete with American wives acquired by members of *Old Shiny's* crew during their ten months stay.

Work to prepare *Sheffield* for the Far East was carried out at Portsmouth, but before she could set sail, American B-29 Superfortress bombers dropped two atomic bombs on Hiroshima and Nagasaki, curtailing the war by an estimated six months.

In her five years of war HMS *Sheffield* had sailed a quarter of a million miles and, during her first year, spent two thirds of her time at sea. Her record of twelve battle honours being beaten only by the battleship *Warspite,* that had gained two of its thirteen at Jutland and Matapan in World War One, and the cruiser *Orion* also with thirteen. The name *Sheffield* had only existed with the Royal Navy for eight years, but had already gained her position in history.

King George VI on board Sheffield with Rear Admiral Bob Burnett on the right of the picture and Admiral Bruce Fraser standing behind the King, May 11th 1944.
(Photo: H.M.S.S.A)

H.M.S. Sheffield 1946 (Photo: H.M.S.S.A)

The Post War Years
West Indian Guard Ship

By November 1946 the war had been over for a month and *Sheffield* had been in refit for seventeen months at Portsmouth. Some of the crew wondered whether *Sheffield* would sail again as many ships of the fleet were facing the scrapyard.

However, on Wednesday November 14th Captain Kenneth Harkness arrived. With so much work being carried out between 1944 and 1946 it had been decided that *Sheffield* should serve as flagship of the North American and West Indian Fleet.

Sheffield would be the first Royal Navy warship to start a peace time commission. By March 1946 *Old Shiny* was almost ready. Captain Harkness invited Princess Marina, Duchess of Kent who had launched *Sheffield* ten years earlier to lunch aboard while she was inspecting the Wrens at Portsmouth. The Princess asked if Lieutenant Philip Mountbatten could accompany her. Captain Harkness did not know who this Prince Philip of Greece was, but it wasn't his place to question.

Berthed at Malta, on the way South, 1946 (Photo: H.M.S.S.A)

Sheffield arrived in Bermuda on August 30th 1946. On her way she had gone to Malta to 'work up' her crew. Bermuda was to be *Sheffield's* base during her spell as West Indian guard ship. The base called *HMS Malaban* was small and *Sheffield* was the flagship of a fleet that comprised the cruiser *Kenya* and the frigates *Porlock Bay* and *Padstow Bay*.

For the rest of the year *Sheffield* went on a tour of the West Indies calling at Nassau, Kingston, Trinidad, Grenada, Barbados and Antigua. Returning to Bermuda on October 15th she spent the next three weeks in dry dock for minor repairs.

December saw a new Captain, Fawkes, and with a name like this he was often referred to as 'Guy'. There wasn't much in terms of a New Year holiday for *Sheffield's* crew as she left Bermuda on New Years Day for her winter cruise. During January the ship visited Jamaica, Colon (Peru), Balkoa, Antofagasta and Valparaiso (Chile). Six days were spent at Port Stanley in the Falkland Islands from where she sailed to Montevideo where the ship's Royal Marine band took part in the inaugural parade of the newly elected President of Uruguay.

The most interesting visit of this tour occurred on March 7th when *Sheffield* visited Buenos Aires. There President Juan Peron and his wife Eva came aboard as guests of Admiral William Termet, Commander in Chief of the North

American and West Indies fleet. *Sheffield* returned to Bermuda on April 15th after visiting ports in Brazil and Venezuela. She had steamed 13,000 miles in just over 3 months.

For summer 1947 *Sheffield* was to head northward arriving at Halifax, Canada on July 1st. En route to Peter Arm, Newfoundland the ship came across an iceberg that was used by the Marine Manned Secondary Armament as target practice. They scored a number of direct hits!

Right: Captain 'Guy' Fawkes, Sheffield's commander 1946-48.
Below: Iceberg near Newfoundland used as target practice for Shiny's 4-inch guns
(Photos: Vic Chappel)

At St. Johns, Newfoundland the ship's company decided to hold a party for around one hundred orphan children, but in error the local radio station announced that *HMS Sheffield* was throwing a Children's Party that resulted in over two thousand kids turning up. Rapid changes to catering had to be made! *Sheffield* arrived at New York in September to be welcomed by Jewish protests about alleged anti-Jewish policies of the British Government.

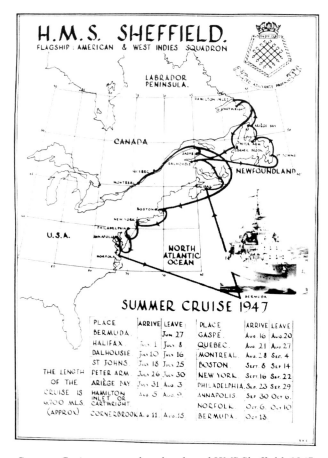

Summer Cruise map produced on board HMS Sheffield, 1947

PHILADELPHIA TRANSPORTATION COMPANY

THIS PASS PERMITS A UNIFORMED OFFICER OR
MEMBER OF CREW OF

H. M. S. SHEFFIELD

TO USE STREET CAR, SUBWAY-ELEVATED OR BUS LINES OF

PHILADELPHIA TRANSPORTATION CO.

FROM SEPTEMBER 23 TO SEPTEMBER 29, 1947, INCLUSIVE

699

PRESIDENT

(This permit will be shown to Conductor or Cashier in lieu of payment of fare)

Free travel pass issued during Sheffield's visit to Philadelphia

After visiting Philadelphia, Aunapoli and Norfolk, *Sheffield* returned to Bermuda on October 13th.

She took New Years Day 1948 off, but sailed on the 2nd for her winter cruise, starting with Marana, Cuba on January 5th. After a visit to New Orleans, she was ordered to proceed as fast as possible to Belize (British Honduras) as there was a threat of invasion from neighbouring Guatemala. She arrived on February 2nd.

Two Bofors 40mm anti-aircraft guns were removed from *Sheffield* and placed on trucks. The ship's Royal Marines took these to the airport where they dug in for attack. However, after a couple of days the Guatemalens withdrew and all went back to normal.

After visiting places such as Jamaica, Barbados and Antigua, *Sheffield* docked at Bermuda in April having covered

One of Sheffield's 40mm Bofors guns mounted on a truck in defence of Belize

Tents of Shiny's Royal Marines defending Belize's airport (Photos: Vic Chappel)

Floodlit in harbour (Photo: Vic Chappel)

Passing through one of the locks on the Panama Canal. To the left the little railway engines can be seen that pull ships through the locks (Photo: A.Cooke)

6,318 miles from January 2nd to April 6th 1948. During the Summer of 1948 *Sheffield* passed through the Panama Canal and arrived at Acapulco in Mexico on July 17th. Throughout the summer she gradually worked her way up the west coast of America, visiting the Canadian city of Vancouver in August. *Sheffield* returned to Bermuda on October 4th, but was hastily dispatched to act as meteorological report ship during a hurricane which was hitting the West Indies. Considerable damage was sustained with the ship being thrown ten miles off course.

Storm damage October 7th 1948. Breakwater pulled from its mountings (Photos: Vic Chappel)

Smashed to bits. Another one of Sheffield's wooden boats

86

Above: Ship's company 1946-49

Right: Transferring the King's colours to HMS Glasgow, Sheffield's sister ship. Glasgow was taking over as West Indies guard ship, October 24th 1948
(Photos: Vic Chappel)

The commission over, *Sheffield* was relieved by her sister ship *Glasgow* and set sail for home. Home was reached on November 5th with the ship arriving at Chatham. This being quite an appropriate date considering the Captain's name!

At the beginning of 1949 *Sheffield* was paid off and placed in refit which was to take two years.

Tony Richardson's birthday on Old Shiny.
Typical post war mess deck scene (Photo: A.E.Richardson)

Back to the West Indies

In March 1951 *Sheffield* re-commissioned under the command of Captain Michael Everhard. One of her first jobs was to take King George and Queen Elizabeth from Liverpool to Belfast. However, the King was ill suffering from lung cancer so Princess Margaret took his place.

In early October *Sheffield* left for Bermuda to again become flagship of the West Indian fleet, with Vice Admiral Sir William Andrew as Commander in Chief. However, the naval base at Bermuda at this point was run down. Most of the shipyard workers had returned to the UK and the base was a ghost town.

Initially *Sheffield* carried out exercises with the US Navy docking at Norfolk, Virginia on November 23rd. *Sheffield's* sailors were struck by the flashiness of the town compared to rationed England. The US Navy laid on buses for two hundred crew members to visit Williamsburg which had been the seat of British Colonial Administration before 1776.

Next she visited Baltimore where a kids' party was laid on and around eight thousand people visited the ship. *Sheffield* was illuminated, with the marine band supplying pomp by performing the ceremony of Beat The Retreat which included precision marching that dated back some three hundred years. Wherever possible, *Sheffield's* sports team would compete with local teams. In Baltimore the ship's football team played against a local college team. Sadly *Sheffield* was beaten 5 - 0.

Four days later *Sheffield* returned to Bermuda. It was Christmas and the Lord Mayor of the capital, Hamilton, invited *HMS Sheffield* and her ship's company to spend the holiday period at the city's principal quay. The Bermuda Royal Gazette proclaimed 'Welcome awaits Royal Navy Men'. Floodlit at night *Sheffield* was centre to the four thousand residents of Hamilton and dances were held with the Royal Marine band playing.

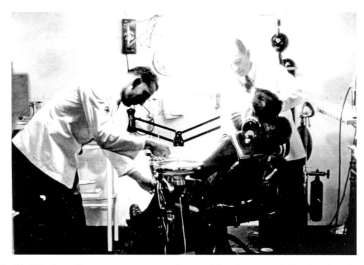

Sheffield's dental surgery was very advanced for the period. During her time on the West Indies station many foreign dentists requested to visit her facilities to see what was new (Photo: H.M.S.S.A)

Sheffield returned to the Naval dockyard on December 29th and left for her winter cruise to the West Indies on January 4th, five days later dropping anchor off Antigua. One hundred sailors visited the English Harbour which was reckoned to be the most beautiful harbour in the world. Closing down in 1889 it had been used by the ships of Nelson.

After Antigua, *Sheffield* visited Barbados where the local aquatic club threw a dance for the ship's company. Many locals welcomed sailors in to their homes and generally a good time was had by all.

Mainland South America was *Shiny's* next stop. In Venezuela two hundred of the crew visited the capital, Caracus, three hundred feet above sea level and home to a quarter of a million people. On the last day of the visit *Sheffield* was opened to visitors, but the crew were warned not to 'make eyes' at the local girls as the local lads were somewhat 'hot blooded'.

Williamsland, the capital of Curaçao was the next port of call, arriving on February 6th 1952. Unfortunately, this was the day that King George VI died. Some crew members were sickened at the news, not only for the sad loss of the King, but because it also meant that the next part of the cruise would be cancelled.

It had been planned that *Sheffield* would pass through the Panama Canal and the Pacific Ocean to meet the Royal Yacht and escort Princess Elizabeth home after her expected visit to Australia. The Princess would now make a quick departure from Africa by plane. New Orleans was supposed to be the highlight of the cruise visiting during Mardi Gras. For a few days *Sheffield* lay at Curaçao with flags at half mast before moving on to Jamaica. Errol Flynn, the actor, owned a small island off Jamaica and came aboard *Sheffield* with his wife, mother and father.

Montreal, Canada where Sheffield was opened up to the masses, May 23rd 1952
(Photo: H.M.S.S.A)

In March *Sheffield* visited the US Naval Base of Guantanama, Cuba. After the customary return to Bermuda, *Sheffield* left for the colder climate of Canada. Montreal was the destination, with a stop at Halifax on the way. At Halifax *Sheffield* was guest of the Canadian Navy with much drink laid on and tours of the city.

At Montreal 14,000 people came aboard *Sheffield* including some Red Indians in full dress to entertain the crew with their dancing. Then it was back to Bermuda where there had been little rainfall for some time. *Sheffield* was able to produce 30,000 gallons of fresh water for the population from her own water making machines.

On the first day of July *Sheffield* left for her final cruise of the commission to visit the Pacific coast of America. She arrived in San Francisco on July 21st 1952 and was greeted by an earthquake that killed nine people. However, *Sheffield* had a fun filled eight days before sailing to Seattle and then to Canadian Vancouver Island where another 10,000 visitors came to her. *Old Shiny* then sailed up the Columbia River flanked by green forests to visit Portland, Oregon, USA a city of a half a million people. Many of *Sheffield's* crew considered that Portland was the best visit of the cruise with perfect weather, friendly locals and pretty girls!

A couple of farewell incidents had the crew and locals laughing. One of the ship's Petty Officers, looking worse for wear, arrived on the quay in a siren screaming police car, but sadly he was too late. *Sheffield* had just cast off. Also, whilst passing under one of the bridges on the way out of Portland a lady dropped a garland of flowers on the ship for one of the crew she had encountered. The poor sailor in question had the embarrassment of collecting the flowers in front of eight hundred of his ship mates!

Three days later, to a 21-gun salute, *Sheffield* entered the Californian Naval Base of San Pedro. The base was four miles from Long Beach and twenty miles from Hollywood.

One day during *Sheffield's* stay the officers held a cocktail party which film stars Walter Pidgeon, Ronald Coleman, Stewart Grainger and his wife Jean Simmons attended. Buses were laid on for the crew to visit the film studios of Hollywood. Some sailors there had been invited to spend a day at Grainger's house.

Sheffield finally called at San Diego before sailing away from the United States on September 22nd to head for Acapulco, Mexico.

Sheffield's famous visitors
between 1952 and 1953
(Photos: Northern Film Poster Archive)

Left: Jean Simmons

Below: Errol Flynn

The ship's company, November 30th 1953, with the newly crowned Queen, Elizabeth II central at the front, Prince Philip to her left and Lord Louis Mountbatten to her right. Taken at Kingston, Jamaica (Photo: H.M.S.S.A)

Mexico was intended to be the last port of call on the cruise, but instead of passing through the Panama Canal, *Sheffield* was held for ten days at Balloa. It transpired that *Sheffield* was the only British vessel in the area and British presence was required for the inauguration of the new Chilean President at Santiago, the country's capital. After a detachment of the crew with the band had given the Chileans some pomp and glory, it was off home for *Old Shiny*.

After brief fuel stops at Jamaica and Bermuda, *Sheffield* arrived back home at Portsmouth after being away for fourteen months.

HMS Sheffield after her refit 1957 (Photo: Ann Diver)

Final Commission 1957-59

Sheffield had been refitting at Chatham for six months where £1.5 million was spent on her. At last, after twenty years, she was fitted with an enclosed bridge. A new main mast was fitted complete with all the latest radar and pre-wetting equipment was fitted to counter nuclear fall-out. Formica was fitted internally to assist cleaning.

On July 1st 1957 *Old Shiny* re-commissioned under the command of Captain Bourke of the New Zealand Navy. In August the ship paid her second and last visit to Immingham, the closest she could get to Sheffield. 8,000 people from the city visited the ship, with a contingent of crew visiting Sheffield in return.

Sailing on September 17th, *Old Shiny* was to take part in one of the largest NATO exercises held up to that point, along with the cruiser *Gambia* and the 4th Destroyer Squadron. Then she joined a large task group which included the American carrier *Essex* and the battleship *Iowa*.

The object at this stage of the exercise was to run through the Iceland Faroes gap to a position off Norway. The sea was infested with submarines and intelligence informed the crew that it was with regret that they were to announce to *Sheffield* that she had been, theoretically, sunk by one.

In November the ship visited the German port of Bremen where thousands of Germans came on board. The crew was impressed with the vibrance and wealth of a country that they had been at war with just twelve years earlier.

August 4th 1957, Sheffield arrives at Immingham

Crew members from the City of Sheffield, from left to right: Writer Harry Diver, Jack Townsend, Peter Ridgeway and Tony Hatcliffe (Photos: Ann Diver)

Above: Heavy Seas at Cape Wrath, Scottish waters, Exercise 'Strikeback'. Gambia follows

Left: Firing a torpedo, 1957

Below: The anti-submarine frigate Keppel refuels from Sheffield (Photos: Ann Diver)

Many will have heard of the maritime tradition of 'Crossing the Line' where, as a ship crosses the equator, people who pass the latitude for the first time are ducked in front of King Neptune.

Not so well known is the ritual of passing into the Arctic Circle, latitude 67 degrees North. During exercise 'Strikeback' Sheffield was visited by 'His Majesty of the Northern Realms', King Polar Bear and his Queen, Aurora Borealis. Above in conversation with Captain Bourke and below with their entourage of penguins. Does his highness look rather like one of the Old Shiny's Petty Officers? *(Photos: Ann Diver)*

Bremen, Germany with the frigate Scarborough, November 1957

German visitors flood on board (Photos: Ann Diver)

Refuelling at Sea from a Royal Fleet Auxiliary (RFA)

By January 1958, *Sheffield* was back at her familiar home of Gibraltar and in February at Malta. March saw her visiting Yugoslavia, docking for a five day goodwill visit at Split.

January 1958, Gibraltar (Photos: Ann Diver)

The Final Years 1960-67

In reserve, Portsmouth, Whale Island (Photo: M.P.L.)

After her final commission *Old Shiny* was placed in reserve at Portsmouth. She was to become the flagship of the reserve fleet replacing the Royal Navy's last battleship, *Vanguard,* in 1960. Officially *Sheffield* remained at seven days readiness for sea, retaining only a small crew for maintenance.

During the Navy Days of August 1963 *Sheffield* was still the star attraction due to her wartime fame. Apart from her half sister, *Belfast,* all her surviving sisters had long been scrapped. *Old Shiny* was one of the last of a dying breed.

The days of cruisers in the British Navy were also drawing to a close. Since the end of the war only three new cruisers had been completed. These were the Tiger class vessels; *Tiger, Blake* and *Lion* built using hulls started during the war but incomplete by 1945. Finished as state of the art in 1959 they were considered obsolete by the mid 1960's. Technology was moving fast.

By 1966, with the talk being of guided missiles, nuclear submarines and computerisation, *Old Shiny* now of four decades was past her best. *Belfast,* last of the wartime cruisers, was to take *Sheffield's* place in the reserve fleet. Attempts were made to preserve *Old Shiny* but they failed.

In January 1967, *Sheffield* left Portsmouth under tow to Rosyth so that she could be stripped of re-useable items. Finally on September 18th 1967 *Old Shiny* made her last voyage under tow to Faslane, Clydeside to be broken up. Within six months she was no more.

Once the pride of the Navy (Photo: M.P.L.)

Of her steel, around one thousand tons of her quality armour plate found its way to the City of Sheffield to be melted down and used again. The remaining steel went to Scottish steelworks to find its way into thousands of different items. Maybe your kitchen sink helped sink the *Bismarck!*

The last voyage. After thirty years tugs tow the old veteran to the scrapyard (Photo: M.P.L.)

Above: At the breakers, silent and gun-less, September 1967
Below: The last day in the water, the last picture, the end of Old Shiny, October 2nd 1968
(Photos: H.M.S.S.A.)

By 1971 the end had also come for *HMS Belfast* and this was the last of the line. There were no more battleships, no more battle cruisers. *Sheffield's* half sister was the last of the 'big gun' Royal Navy ships of the 20th Century and so she became the first warship, since Nelson's *Victory*, to be preserved for the nation. She is a memorial to 50,758 men who died and 22,884 wounded in service in the Royal Navy during the Second World War.

Considering how few warships are preserved owing to cost and space, we are fortunate that Sheffield's larger half sister, HMS Belfast, is maintained for the nation in the Pool of London. Although extensively rebuilt in the 1950's she does give a good insight to what Old Shiny was like to serve in (Photo: Author)

Today *Old Shiny's* stainless steel bell hangs proudly in Sheffield Cathedral. Her battle ensign and cast badge are also mounted in St. George's chapel a few metres away. In 1969 a new pub opened at Lodge Moor in Sheffield. Named the *Shiny Sheff* it is full of pictures of *Old Shiny* and exhibits a three foot model of the cruiser.

Ensign made by Sheffield ladies in 1937. Stainless steel bell and badge, all now on display in Sheffield Cathedral (Photos: Author)

Jet Powered Wonder-Ship
The Second HMS Sheffield

Although the second *Sheffield* did not enter service until 1975 her design and size dated back to 1966. In this year the Royal Navy was ordering a class of new large aircraft carriers, code-named CVA-01, to replace four ships that dated back to World War Two. In order to protect these valuable ships a class of large destroyer Type 82 was planned.

Eight of these Bristol Class destroyers were planned. Weighing 6,750 tons they were almost as big as a wartime light cruiser with hull and engines derived from the successful County Class destroyers, the first of which, *Devonshire,* had entered service in 1963. The main armament was the Sea Dart missile (originally known as CF299) which could shoot down a target forty miles away. Developed and manufactured by British Aerospace, initial work started in 1962 with test firings commencing in 1965. The missile cruises at about Mach 3.5 and was intended for use against attacking aircraft and missiles.

What HMS Sheffield should have looked like. The sole Type 82 destroyer, HMS Bristol
(Photo: Henry Hudson)

Additionally the Bristol Class were to be equipped with a single rapid fire 4½"
gun and the Australian Ikara anti-submarine missile, giving the ship area
defence capabilities to protect a future carrier group.

However, 1966 saw a new Labour government and with it vast defence cuts
leading to cancellation of many projects, from the Royal Air Force's TSR2 to
the Royal Navy's CVA-01 aircraft carriers. The argument was that, not only
could Britain no longer afford such high defence spending, but that in the case
of CVA-01 the new era of anti-ship missiles and nuclear weapons would make
such a large target a sitting duck. Also in consideration was that with the end of
the Empire and the moving of Britain to the defence of NATO countries in the
West, the need for aircraft operating from ships at sea was minimal.

With the loss of CVA-01 there was no longer a need for the Type 82 destroyers,
so all but one were cancelled. The one sole remaining ship was named *Bristol*
and was intended for development for both Sea Dart and Ikara systems. *HMS
Bristol* entered service in 1973.

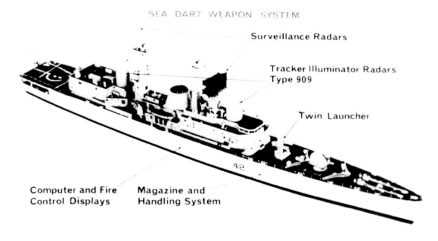

*An early model of the 'Sheffield Class'. Note the Leander class frigate
style superstructure originally intended for the Type 42's*

With severe cash constraints in force the Royal Navy decided that it was able to
pick up the pieces of its cancelled projects and produce a somewhat smaller
new class of area defence destroyer for the 1970's. With advancements in
electronics, making radar and missile systems smaller and more automated,
space could be saved. In terms of propulsion the Navy had, for around 50 years,

110

used steam turbines with large boilers and turbines. The ships would therefore have boiler rooms and engine rooms not only occupying much space, but also requiring vast crews to man them. In July 1968 the Royal Navy began trials of gas turbines fitted in a converted frigate *HMS Exmouth*. The engines, one Olympus (same as Concorde) and two Proteus, had their centre shafts directly connected to the propellers via gearboxes.

The second Sheffield takes shape at Vickers, Barrow in Furness 1969/70
(Photo: H.M.S.S.A.)

What resulted was a single engine room requiring few crew with the possibility of controlling the engines from the bridge. With the experiment being successful it was decided to fit two Tyne and two Olympus gas turbine engines into the new destroyers. The ship would cruise with these engines giving high speed performance over 30 knots. The weight was reduced by some 3,000 tons to 3,660 tons.

On November 14th 1968 the first of these new Type 42 guided missile destroyers was ordered from Vickers. She was to become the second *HMS Sheffield,* launched by Her Majesty the Queen on Thursday June 10th 1971. Her construction was marred by the death of a shipyard worker who died in a fire on board. Ironically, Vickers was building another Type 42 destroyer for the Argentine Navy at the same time. As a goodwill gesture the Argentines allowed parts from their new ship to be removed and fitted to *Sheffield* in order that her construction should not be delayed.

The Queen launches the second Royal Navy warship to bear the name Sheffield. The first member of the Type 42 'Sheffield' class
(Photo: Sheffield Newspapers)

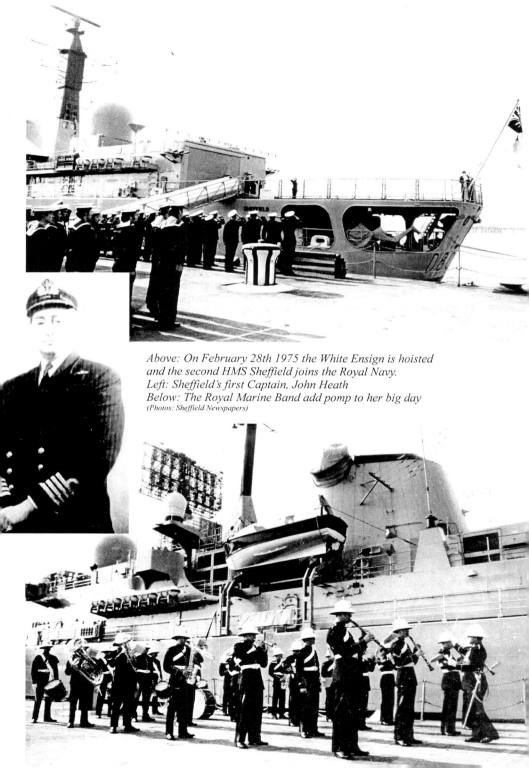

Above: On February 28th 1975 the White Ensign is hoisted and the second HMS Sheffield joins the Royal Navy.
Left: Sheffield's first Captain, John Heath
Below: The Royal Marine Band add pomp to her big day
(Photos: Sheffield Newspapers)

When the second Sheffield was commissioned, four of her crew had served in Old Shiny. These were, from left to right: Petty Officer Ray Whintle, Petty Officer Ray Holland of Rivelin Valley, Sheffield, Commander G. Hitchens and Petty officer Pete Hollby from York (Photo: Sheffield Newspapers)

Silver coasters presented to the ship by The Sheffield Telegraph
(Photo: Sheffield Newspapers)

HMS Sheffield, 1977
(Photo: B Briscoe)

Sheffield's 'teeth': the twin Sea Dart missile launcher complete with two missiles
(Photo: Sheffield Newspapers)

Below: Whereas Old Shiny had twelve 6-inch guns and eight 4-inch guns the second Sheffield had this single 4½-inch gun. However, it could fire a shell the same distance as Old Shiny's main 6-inch guns and with far greater accuracy. This turret was totally automated, the bodywork was glassfibre with no armour.
(Photo: Author)

Sheffield at sea with the experimental Royal Navy hovercraft
(Photo: B. Briscoe)

The second *Sheffield* joined the Navy on February 28th 1975 when she commissioned at Portsmouth. Attending were dignitaries from the City of Sheffield and, being the first of a new generation of warship, she was given much publicity. The press referred to her as the first in a new generation of jet ships. She was of course powered by the same Rolls Royce jet engines as Concorde!

Being the first of a new class, *Sheffield* spent many of her first few years conducting trials and evaluations. Her systems were tested in hot weather conditions in the Caribbean and her performance was evaluated in cold weather off Bear Island, Norway. Everything from weapons to air conditioning was tested. Her air conditioning plant maintained a steady temperature of 68° Fahrenheit, whatever the outside conditions. Her Sea Dart missiles destroyed an airborne target with the first firing on the Aberporth missile range in Cardigan Bay.

Sheffield attended the Queen's Silver Jubilee Naval Review at Spithead, Portsmouth in 1977 and was allocated to the Third Destroyer Squadron, again at Portsmouth.

Sheffield at speed with the first Type 21 frigate, Amazon. A Navy Sea King helicopter is between the two, 1974.
(Photo: B. Briscoe)

Moored at Spithead in 1977 for the Queen's Silver Jubilee Review of the fleet (Photo: M.P.L.)

Most of the next two years were spent in North European waters ending with an attachment to the NATO Standing Force in the Atlantic. This multi-national fleet of warships maintained a constant patrol against the Soviet threat.

Sheffield leads the Leander class frigate Ariadne and the USS Paul during her time with NATO Standing Force, 1979 (Photo: R.N.)

Doing around 30 knots. Above whilst under trials, 1974 and below during the late 1970's. Sheffield could be distinguished from her sisters due to having exhaust outlets either side of the funnel. These were intended to divert the hot exhaust gases away from the radar on the main mast. However, plans were made to remove these during her mid-life refit in the mid 1980's (Photos: B. Briscoe)

June 14th 1980 two lads from the City of Sheffield are entertained on board Sheffield at a Junior Star Party (Photo: Sheffield Newspapers)

In June 1979 she began her first refit which took over a year until November 1980. During this period the Sheffield Star took a party of local boys to Portsmouth to visit the ship.

After a year in home waters *Sheffield* deployed east to the Indian Ocean as the head of a task group patrolling the entrance to the Persian Gulf. In March 1982 she was taking part in exercises around Gibraltar before returning home in April.

EXOCET

On April 2nd 1982 Argentina invaded the small British dependency known as the Falkland Islands. These islands were about the size of Wales, 8,000 miles from the United Kingdom, but a mere few hundred miles from Argentina. Britain and Argentina had always been good friends, but the issue of the Falklands, or Malvinas as the Argentines called them, was always a thorny one and Argentina claimed sovereignty. In 1981 the defence review carried out by John Nott made savage cuts to the Navy's surface fleet. Amongst them the ice patrol ship *HMS Endurance* was to be scrapped after her 1982 South Atlantic patrol. This was seen by the Argentine Junta as an open invitation and that the British had lost interest in the Falklands.

Sheffield was near Gibraltar on her way home. She had been away for six months patrolling the Gulf where Iran and Iraq were at war. That day the captain, Sam Salt, came over the ship's tannoy to tell the crew *"Not to worry chaps, we have orders to go home arriving on April 6th as planned"*. However a mere six hours later he unfortunately had to tell the crew *"Forget what I said. We're steaming south"*

It is understood that the crew were not too bothered about their leave being delayed as most considered that the crisis would be over before they reached Ascension Island.

On the way south four of the crew entered a Punch magazine contest to win a hand-woven Harris Tweed hat. They wrote a poem:

> **On the Falkland Argentine we sat**
> **Said Maggie "We cannot have that"**
> **When the fleet hove in sight**
> **They were all put to flight**
> **By Sam Salt in his Harris Tweed Hat!**

Sheffield takes on supplies of food and weapons from the supply ship RFA Fort Austin. Above: food supplies. Below: Sea Dart missiles are transferred in their protective cases (Photos: Bob Mahoney)

Sheffield was one of the first ships to arrive at the Falklands. When she arrived there the shooting had yet to start. At that time an exclusion zone was in force, whereby the Argentines had been informed that any ship or aircraft attempting to reach the occupied Falklands Islands would be liable to attack. *Sheffield,* just like her sisters, was forward air defence picket.

What is thought to be the last photograph of HMS Sheffield, having just finished taking on supplies from Fort Austin. The destroyer is turning back to the task force and, unbeknown, into history (Photo: Bob Mahoney)

The *Sheffield* class had been designated as area defence destroyer with their long range type 965 radar intended to spot enemy aircraft many miles away. Her advanced Sea Dart missiles were designed to shoot down supersonic aircraft up to eighty miles away. One disadvantage of her role meant that *Sheffield* and her sisters were positioned in front of the task force on a limb sixty miles nearer Argentina than the rest of the task force.

I remember the day of Tuesday May 4th 1982 very clearly. I was in the fifth form at Silverdale School, Sheffield, about to take my O-level exams. I had taken a keen interest in the Falklands crisis ever since it started, rushing home from school to see what had developed each day through the television news.

That day had seemed quiet. Two days before, the British submarine, *Conqueror* had sunk the Argentinian cruiser *General Belgrano* and it was anticipated that Argentina would seek revenge through her Navy. At 21:00 the BBC broadcast a live transmission from Ian McDonald, the Ministry of Defence spokesperson. I remember his words well:

> ***"During the course of her duties around the total exclusion zone, the Type 42 destroyer HMS Sheffield was hit by an Argentine missile"***

He went on to inform us that fire had spread through the ship and, after eight hours, the ship had been abandoned. With the fires out of control there had been casualties.

I had seen pictures of what anti-ship missiles could do to boats. A ship like the *Sheffield* could expect to lose a third of its crew. In actual fact 21 men died on Sheffield out of a crew of 270. The first picture of the stricken ship showed her remarkably intact, despite billowing out vast quantities of black smoke. The hull peeled away by the blast, rather like a banana. It transpired that *Sheffield* had been struck by a French-made Exocet missile fired at a low level by a French-made Super Etendard aircraft. The missile, flying just a few metres above sea level, had hit *Sheffield* midships, finishing up in her main engine room.

Information that the Royal Navy possessed suggested that, at the time of the Falklands war, Argentina had only received a few Super Etendard aircraft and four or five Exocets which were thought to be far from ready to use, lacking the ability to arm them properly. Hence the Navy did not expect missile attack from these weapons. In fact, technicians from the missile's French manufacturer, Aerospatiale, were still in Argentina advising in a technical capacity at the time of the invasion.

Smoke billows from Sheffield. To the left men in a Gemini rubber boat attempt to spray water directly into the hole caused by the missile. Fuel from her engines' fuel tanks rapidly ignited producing vast quantities of black smoke (Photo: I.W.M Neg FKD66)

Lieutenant Commander Nick Batho, *Sheffield's* air warfare officer, was in the operator's room when the radar picked up a contact, possibly an aircraft coming from the west. It was mid-morning and members of *Sheffield's* crew had been on the telephone to her sister ship, *Coventry*, to talk about false radar images they had been picking up. He informed the Officer of the Watch, Lieutenant Peter Walpole, of the apparent incoming aircraft. The contact had been lost so perhaps it was returning Sea Harriers. Royal Navy ships had trained against the Soviet threat, a threat that gave a twenty minute warning from medium height aircraft firing missiles. However two and a half minutes after Batho had first spotted the 'contact', Walpole and Brian Leyshon, the Lynx helicopter pilot, spotted smoke on the horizon and suddenly realised it was a missile coming their way.

There was only time to order the crew to take cover before the Exocet travelling at 680 mph struck *Sheffield* on her starboard side around nine feet above the waterline. The missile entered the engine room where it destroyed the neighbouring galley and operations room. In the other direction the blast destroyed the machinery control room and damage control HQ.

HMS SHEFFIELD:
The killer blow

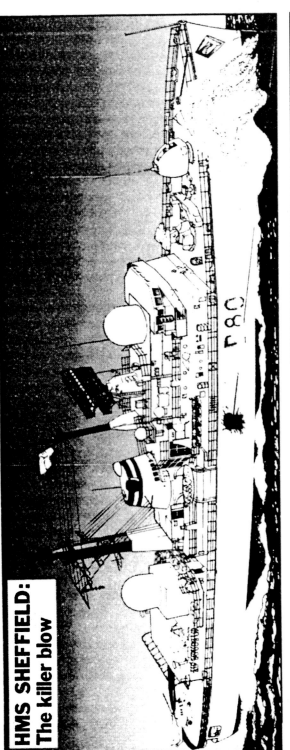

How attacking jets fly under ship's radar

HMS SHEFFIELD

Spotter Etendard | Attacking Etendard

RADAR DEADGROUND

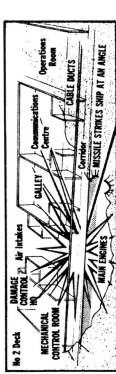

No 2 Deck

MECHANICAL CONTROL ROOM

DAMAGE CONTROL 2 HQ

Air Intakes

GALLEY

Communications Centre

Operations Room

CABLE DUCTS

Corridor

MISSILE STRIKES SHIP AT AN ANGLE

MAIN ENGINES

Contemporary illustration published in The Sunday Times a few days after HMS Sheffield's loss. The lower right drawing shows how the missile cut through the cable ducts leaving Sheffield lifeless. This was a fundamental design fault. Earlier ships, such as the first Sheffield, had all the services buried low down in the centre of the ship, as far away from the outside as possible.

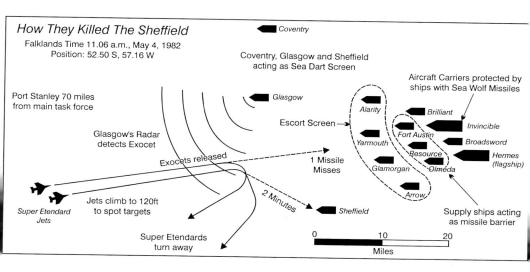

How They Killed The Sheffield

Falklands Time 11.06 a.m., May 4, 1982
Position: 52.50 S, 57.16 W

Coventry, Glasgow and Sheffield
acting as Sea Dart Screen

Aircraft Carriers protected by
ships with Sea Wolf Missiles

Coventry

Glasgow

Alarity

Brilliant

Escort Screen →

Invincible

Fort Austin

Port Stanley 70 miles
from main task force

Yarmouth

Broadsword

Glasgow's Radar
detects Exocet

Resource

Hermes
(flagship)

Exocets released

1 Missile
Misses

Glamorgan

Olmeda

Super Etendard
Jets

Jets climb to 120ft
to spot targets

2 Minutes

Arrow

Sheffield

Supply ships acting
as missile barrier

Super Etendards
turn away

0   10   20

Miles

Luckily, as the attack had come so quickly, the Officer of the Watch, Walpole,
had no time to bring the vessel back to 'action stations' and hence saved many
lives as most of the crew were asleep at the rear of the ship.

A casualty comes aboard the aircraft carrier Hermes (Photo: I.W.M. Neg FKD213)

Unluckily, with the engine room ablaze, *Sheffield* had lost all power which was needed for propulsion, lighting and to pump water to fight the fire. Normally a back-up generator would provide emergency power. Made by GEC, the Paxman Ventura Diesel is the same engine that powers Britain's High Speed Train, but in *Sheffield's* case the generator was not working, awaiting spares. Rapidly smoke from intense fires spread throughout the ship. The crew tried to control the smoke by closing water-tight doors, but found that many would not close due to distortion caused by the force of the impact. Soon, Sam Salt had to order any crew members not fighting the fire to go on deck, away from the smoke. The bridge filled with acrid black smoke and had to be evacuated. It became clear that most of the casualties had been in the galley and the computer room below the operations room. Injured crew were flown by helicopter to the flagship *Hermes* suffering with burns and smoke injuries. Some had up to 60% burns and survived.

Back on *Sheffield,* crew were even using buckets of water to try to fight the fire. Mobile pumps had been brought on board and some crew members tried spraying water through the hole in the ship from a Gemini rubber boat. All the efforts were in vain. Much of the water turned to steam due to the intense heat. Even in fire-fighting suits with breathing apparatus the heat was still too intense and visibility inside was zero. On the above decks the heat was melting the soles of crew members' shoes. After four and a half hours, Sam Salt realised how desperate things were. Even if the fires were controlled, *Sheffield* was damaged too severely to be of any use to the task force. It would take months of dockyard work to get her operational again.

The task force had deployed *Arrow* and *Yarmouth* to aid *Sheffield.* Sam Salt was concerned about diverting resources away from the task force to try to save *Sheffield.* He was more concerned about how close the fire and heat were getting to the magazines where the 22 Sea Dart missiles and around 150 4½ inch shells were kept. In Naval history the cases of *Hood* and *Barham* show that when a ship's magazine explodes few crew survive. It transpired, afterwards, that the magazines were flooded with water, but this was not known at the time.

The hole made by the Exocet missile. A crew member vainly tackles the flames (Photo: H.M.S.S.A.)

Apparently, word 'Exocet' is taken from Latin for flying fish

HMS Arrow assists spraying water on to Sheffield's white hot hull. With all power lost, only the 20mm guns either side of the bridge were left operational (Photo: H.M.S.S.A.)

Most of *Sheffield's* crew were on the bow trying to keep their spirits up by, amongst other things, singing the Monty-Python tune 'Always look on the bright side of life'!

So, sadly, Sam Salt gave the order to abandon ship, a hard thing for a sailor to do as the ship is not only their place of work, but also their home. Some sailors jumped into the sea, but *HMS Arrow*, the Type 21 frigate came alongside her allowing *Sheffield's* remaining crew to jump ship. Amongst those who did not survive were Marine Engineer Limont, Lieutenant Commander David Balfour and John Woodhead, these being three of the four people who had entered the Punch magazine contest which, unbeknown to them, they won. Around 220 of *Sheffield's* crew found themselves on *Arrow*, a ship whose crew normally numbered 170. Many received new clothes from *Arrow's* crew and the galley served 1,200 meals in twelve hours. *Arrow's* commander, Paul Botherstone, paid tribute to his men and those of *HMS Sheffield*:

"That tragic afternoon is commonly felt to have been the shortest seven hours in our lives, it passed so quickly. The overriding impression left upon everyone was the magnificent behaviour of Sheffield's men which has sustained Arrow through the actions of subsequent weeks".

21 of *Sheffield's* men had died. In just a few seconds, more men had died on the second *Sheffield* than the twelve battles and five years of combat of her predecessor.

Everyone thought that the blazing hulk of *Sheffield* would soon blow up. However, the next day the smoking, blackened ship still floated. Men were lowered on to the ship to assess and photograph the damage. The frigate *Yarmouth* took the lifeless *Sheffield* in tow, apparently to South Georgia for further salvage. Six days later in reported heavy seas, *HMS Sheffield* became waterlogged and sank, taking with her the bodies of twenty of her crew.

May 4th 1982 changed the mood of the task force. Before then it had been plain sailing. The Navy realised that a high-tech, state of the art warship costing many millions of pounds could be knocked out by a missile costing mere thousands. Simple machine guns were strapped to railings as a last ditch defence against attack. The Navy had to re-learn the lessons of the Second World War in that its vessels were lacking in close range defence against air attack.

A simple memorial to those lost on board HMS Sheffield stands overlooking the sight where the Exocet hit in 1982 (Photo: H.M.S.S.A.)

Fact, Myth and Legend

The thirty years of *Old Shiny* are supported by much documentation and photographs. Apart from the visit in 1946 of Eva Peron, there is little doubt to her activities.

When it comes to the second *Sheffield* things are different. There are more stories than there are ships in the British Navy! What follows is a brief summary of the stories that I have read about or heard. I will give my opinion, but it will probably take many years before the full truth emerges.

Firstly, there are the shortfalls in *Sheffield's* design. As mentioned before, the earlier Type 42's were a shortened, cut-price version of the Type 82 Bristol class. It was found that, being some fifteen metres shorter than had been intended, these ships were extremely lively in heavy seas, making life uncomfortable for the crew. Reducing the hull length had also reduced the number of Sea Dart missiles the Type 42's could carry. They could only carry 22 missiles. These two shortfalls led the Navy to lengthen the last four of the class improving their stability at sea and increasing their missile stocks.

Secondly, there was the state of the main radar. The type 965, introduced in the 1950's, was considered out of date by the 1970's. The system was gradually being replaced during the time of the Falklands crisis. The 1981 defence review had stated that *Sheffield* and her sisters should not have their radars updated but, in light of the Falklands War, all remaining type 965 radars were replaced by the more modern type 1022.

In terms of myths, firstly it is said that *Sheffield's* computer did not recognise the approaching Exocet because the missile was a NATO type and the computer classed it as 'friendly' and ignored it. I believe that the ship's systems would consider any object that was approaching it at 680 mph as hostile and all reports I have seen indicate that the low flying missile was never spotted by *Sheffield's* radar or computer. *Sheffield's* radar only spotted the Argentine Super Etendard as it 'peeked' over the horizon to get a bearing and range for the attack on *Sheffield*.

The burned out hulk of Sheffield. The whole ship is gutted. Would she have been worth saving?
(Photos:I.W.M.) Neg FKD138 (above), Neg FKD67 (below)

One story states that *Sheffield* didn't see the Exocet as she had turned off her radar in order to communicate with HQ back in the UK. This seems strange as *Sheffield's* duties that day were to be radar picket, positioned in front of the task force to use her radar to give early warning of incoming attacks. Would *Sheffield*, whilst doing such an important job, turn off her eyes just to talk to London? I doubt it. Considering that we know, as mentioned earlier, that *Sheffield's* radar officer had spotted a radar blip, later known to be caused by the Argentine aircraft obtaining a fix on *Sheffield*, we know that the radar was in operation.

That morning the ship was already at 'Action Stations' and Force was surprised at the lack of activity. The on-shore mist and fog was taking a long time to clear and at 13:00, with still no sight of the enemy, the Force Commander ordered the ship to assume the 'Second Degree of Readiness', with half the crew off duty. After all, a ship cannot remain at 'Action Stations' for ever. So with this 'Defence Watch' it was not unreasonable to continue routine administration and communications.

It appears, however, that a fault with the Type 42 destroyer electronics contributed to her end. When signals were being transmitted from the ship via its satellite link, interference was caused at exactly the same frequency as the Agave radar fitted to the Super Etendard aircraft. At the time of attack *Sheffield* was effectively blind. However, this fact was not appreciated until it was too late.

So why did *Sheffield* get hit? The reason appears to be that Argentina was very clever in its use of both its Super Etendard aircraft and her Exocet missiles. Approaching aircraft flying at low level used the curvature of the earth to hide in blind areas beyond view of *Sheffield's* radar. From time to time the attacking aircraft would momentarily 'pop-up' over the horizon to attempt to obtain a radar fix on the target. At this stage the 'pop-up' had to be done rapidly to avoid the intended target spotting them. On *Sheffield*, her radar operator had seen the blip caused by an aircraft 'popping up' but it was too short for her crew to make much from it. Momentary detections on previous days had been put down to twitchy and over-zealous operators so the blip was declared spurious. Also, previous false alarms had left *Sheffield* vitally low of decoy chaff, fired to seduce and distract incoming missiles away from the target.

Apparently, the pilot flying one of the two Super Etendard aircraft, said to be a Yugoslavian mercenary, thought that he had an aircraft carrier on his radar. It was a big target so both aircraft fired their Exocets and turned back home. Once fired, the missiles flew about six to nine feet above sea level. Sheffield's radar

Sheffield under tow by Yarmouth. Why use a valuable asset as a tug?
Perhaps tugs sent down to the South Atlantic had yet to arrive (Photo: I.W.M. Neg FKD214)

didn't work that low hence the first warning she received of her attack was an officer on the bridge seeing a trail of smoke coming from the incoming missile. None of *Sheffield's* shortcomings in size and age of radar could have prevented what happened. There are, in my opinion, only two ways that *Sheffield* could have been saved. Rapidly the Royal Navy realised this and re-learned lessons of fifty years earlier.

Firstly, low flying aircraft making an attack similar to that on *Sheffield* could only be spotted by air-borne radar, carried by an aircraft at an altitude which could look down round the earth's curvature. For many years the Royal Navy had airborne radar aircraft. In the 1950's in the American-supplied Douglas Skyraider and during the 60's and 70's in the Fairey Gannet AEW3. However, these aircraft operated from large aircraft carriers fitted with catapults, the last of which, *Ark Royal,* was withdrawn in 1979.

From then on the fleet lost its eyes, but no-one thought it important as Royal Navy ships would, from now on, operate in seas protected by NATO land based aircraft, or so it was thought.

As *Sheffield* burned, people in the Ministry of Defence knew what had gone wrong. Initially they pondered whether they could get the old Gannet aircraft, which were in storage, to go down to the Falklands in a conventional aircraft carrier with catapult. Although, apparently, the US did offer to lend one of its aircraft carriers it was considered a job that would take too long. An immediate solution was needed. *Hermes* and *Invincible* had no catapults so the only option was to fit a small radar to existing Sea King Helicopters.

Conversion was rapid, two being completed by May 1982 which sailed on the carrier *HMS Illustrious* for the Falklands. However, she arrived too late to see action.

If spotted, *Sheffield* could have engaged her 4.5-inch guns against the Exocet, used her 20mm guns and fired chaff to attempt to decoy the incoming missile. However, her weakness and the whole fleet's weakness was the lack of close range armament. Close range weapons could have defended the ship in the final seconds before impact.

Old Shiny had brimmed with close range weapons, but experts in the 60's considered missiles as the 'be all and end all' and close range weapons to be outdated. In the days following *Sheffield's* loss men strapped any weapon they could find to the ship's railings in a last ditch defence against possible future missile attack.

Post Falklands, all Navy ships were equipped with permanent close range weapons including the American Vulcan Phalanx system that fired over 3,000 bullets a minute at an incoming target. For ships such as the *Sheffield* Class Type 42 destroyers, space was at such a premium that lifeboats had to be removed to allow extra defences to be added.

Today, it is known that the burned-out hulk had not exploded as expected. The frigate *HMS Yarmouth* had taken *Sheffield* in tow. One just wonders why they used a valuable asset like a frigate to tow away the lifeless *Sheffield* when there was at least one Navy tug present in the Falklands. Also the Ministry Of Defence had gone to great trouble to hire commercial tugs, including the powerful East Coast based *Yorkshireman* hired because she was powerful enough to tow any vessel in the Navy, including the carriers *Hermes* and *Invincible*. However, this rumour has since been dispelled, as the Navy confirmed that the tugs had yet to arrive on station.

Officially the initial story told by the MOD was that on May 10th in heavy seas, *HMS Sheffield* began to take in water through the missile entry hole. Enough water flowed on board to make it impossible for *HMS Yarmouth* to reach the safety of South Georgia, where the damaged destroyer could remain until the Falklands War was over. Explosive charges were placed on board *Sheffield* to ensure that she sank in a controlled manner. The BBC reporter, Brian Hanrahan, confirmed this story during a Commons select committee on July 31st 1982. However, at this stage the MOD story had changed to her just sinking in heavy seas, with no mention of explosives being used.

Sheffield loading Sea Darts from Fort Austin.
Were her nuclear weapons off-loaded at the same time? (Photo: Bob Mahoney)

Why so much mystery? Well, almost certainly concerning whether or not *Sheffield* was carrying nuclear weapons on the May 4th 1982. Many Royal Navy ships carried, what is believed to be, a weapon known as WE177, similar to a device used by the RAF as a free fall nuclear bomb. In the Navy WE177 was used as a depth charge dropped by helicopters on suspected submarines.

Sheffield may have had two WE177s stored in proximity to the helicopter hangar, aft of the funnel, not far from where the Exocet blast had occurred and definitely in an area affected by the fire. It is rumoured that *Fort Austin*, a Royal Navy supply vessel, had been given the job of going around the task force picking up nuclear weapons from vessels such as *Sheffield*. David Tinker, who died in the Exocet attack on *Glamorgan* said, in his letter later published after his death, that he had seen dummy nuclear weapons in *Fort Austin's* hangar. *Sheffield* re-supplied from *Fort Austin* just before her loss. Did she off-load her deadly cargo?

If *Sheffield* still had her nuclear weapons on board when she was hit and if these weapons were damaged by the blast or fire, then huge problems could arise from leaking plutonium which they contained. Miles away from home, consigning *Sheffield* to the deep would be the most obvious solution and at least one source has suggested this, even confirming the use of a Mark 8 torpedo in her sinking.

The strangest story so far that I have come across states that *HMS Sheffield* lies in South Georgia Bay, in fifty feet of water, visited annually by Navy divers to inspect her, but they are not allowed to touch her hull!

The facts were, that by World War Two standards, *Sheffield* was a constructive loss, virtually all electrical equipment and cabling destroyed, all machinery destroyed and in the region of 30% of her fabric weakened by intense heat. It is doubtful that her salvage was worthwhile. *Sheffield* was a grave containing twenty of her dead. In the long tradition of the Royal Navy it was more fitting for the *Sheffield* to take her dead to the deep than to face the prospect of the scrapyard.

Tam Dalyell, very much a critic of the Falklands campaign, asked on November 17th 1982 the then Defence Minister Peter Blake whether a salvage team sent to the Falklands was to recover lost nuclear weapons. The reply was that they were there to recover classified items from *HMS Coventry* that had sunk within five minutes, before classified material could be recovered. In terms of *HMS Sheffield* no items had been recovered.

During 1997 and 1998 I have spoken to a number of witnesses who all recount the same story which I currently believe is the truth. *Sheffield* was not carrying nuclear weapons when she was hit. Whether they were removed just before the Exocet hit or when she'd last carried nuclear weapons I cannot determine. The fire had done too much damage and when the ship began to flood in heavy seas whilst under tow there was no option but to aid the sinking process by placing explosive charges on board her. Many times in history the Navy has assisted the end of crippled ships by means of torpedoes or gunfire. Examples include *Old Shiny's* sisters *Manchester,* crippled in enemy waters in the Mediterranean in 1941, and *Edinburgh,* badly damaged whilst on Russian convoy duty, left powerless but afloat only to be sunk by a British torpedo. A crippled ship can be a burden to an overstretched force.

The exact truth will not emerge for years as the relevant documents are classified under the thirty and fifty year rules, but my research seems to indicate that there is no cover up about the end of *HMS Sheffield.*

A City Mourns

The BBC Nine O'Clock News on May 4th seems to be when most people heard of *Sheffield's* fate. Martin Dawes, of the Sheffield Star, on hearing the news joined his colleagues back at work at The Star to produce a special four page supplement.

The apparent rapidness of *Sheffield's* end seemed to shock the city. In sea battles of old, ships would engage each other for hours and even days in the case of *Bismarck*. However, *Sheffield* was crippled within minutes.

Sheffield Cathedral packed for the memorial service to the second HMS Sheffield. Relatives of those lost attended. To the left out of the picture hangs Old Shiny's battle ensign
(Photo: Sheffield Newspapers)

June 1st, 1982. Celebrity cricket match for the HMS Sheffield fund at Abbeydale Park. Attending were Geoff Boycott and Chris Old (Photo: Sheffield Newspapers)

In the Brincliffe Oaks public house at Nether Edge in Sheffield, the landlord, Mike Sharman, collected £36 from his regulars. This was the very beginning of the *HMS Sheffield* Appeal Fund. Rapidly, with much local support, the fund took off. The Star printed a colour poster of the ship that sold for £1, proceeds of which went to the fund. The former Lord Mayor, Enid Hattersley, who had been host to *Sheffield's* crew on one of the visits, backed the fund.

Sheffield Wednesday Football Club donated £100; Sheffield United Football Club £50; Atkinsons, the last independent department store in Sheffield, donated £250. A former captain of *Sheffield*, Pete Erskine, gave £100. Donations varied in amounts from three year old Benjamin Clark who gave his week's pocket money of 10p, to £1,000 from Hugh Seaman.

Sheffield's nightlife also helped: Max Omae, who in 1982 owned Maximillions Night Club, organised a fund raising event on May 28th. Max had attended a cocktail party on *HMS Sheffield* in 1981 and felt he'd lost personal friends from *Sheffield*. George Welste, who ran the Lyceum Theatre at that time, organised 2 nights of Stan Barstow's 'Kind of Loving' in aid of the fund. Napoleon's Casino ran a buffet night raising £1,750.

A Royal Navy cycle team that had arrived at Sheffield Town Hall from Portsmouth, HMS Sheffield's home base.

A local survivor of HMS Sheffield with his parents.
Andrew Stevenson's homecoming May 27th 1982 (Photos: Sheffield Newspapers)

May 1984, Councillor David Blunkett, Lord Mayor Peter Jones and Sam Salt unveil a memorial plaque to the second HMS Sheffield (Photo: Sheffield Newspapers)

Les Vickers held an activity night on May 11th at Turn Ups. His business included ship-breaking and he was able to supply memorabilia from the aircraft carrier *Ark Royal* that they were currently breaking up.

Sheffield Council and Portsmouth Council each donated £100. George Basset, the confectioners, donated £500. Navy sailors cycled from Portsmouth, the home port of *Shiny Sheff,* to raise money and, rather interestingly, a Special Constable from the Atomic Energy base at Warrington, Cheshire carried out a twenty-six mile walk across the Peak District in the hope of raising £2,000.

On May 10th 1982, the day that *Sheffield* finally sank, a memorial service was held at Sheffield Cathedral. Attending amongst the many dignitaries were Mrs Audrey Till, widow of Acting Chief Michael Till and Mrs Jay Norman, widow of Petty Officer Antony Norman.

By May 28th the *HMS Sheffield* appeal fund had reached £43,408. The Polish Club on Ecclesall Road donated £180. Abbeydale Sports Centre organised a charity cricket match that included celebrities such as Geoff Boycott and Chris Old. The fund finally closed after raising £130,000.

Serving on *Sheffield* during the Falklands War was one person from Sheffield, Andrew Stephenson, who survived injuries from the attacks. He returned to a hero's welcome.

September 1997 saw the launch of an appeal by The HMS Sheffield Association to raise £70,000 in order to commission a permanent memorial to all those who died on *HMS Sheffield*.

The Third HMS Sheffield
"The Shiniest of all the Shiny Sheffs"

Sometimes in the Royal Navy a name may remain dormant for years, decades or even centuries. At the time of the loss of the second *Sheffield,* the Navy had stated that they had no intention of reviving the name *Sheffield,* nor that of her sister ship *Coventry* in the foreseeable future.

Public opinion, however, caused the Navy to change its mind and, thus, on May 29th 1984, the keel of the third *HMS Sheffield* was laid down at Swan Hunters shipyard on the Tyne.

This new *Shiny* was to be a frigate, the second batch of the Type 22 Broadsword Class. Designed to replace the well known Leander class, *Sheffield's* main role would be anti-submarine. Ironically, part of her main armament was to be the Exocet missile system, the same French-made system that had destroyed her predecessor.

Larger than the second *Sheffield,* the new ship would also carry the battle proven Seawolf missile, an excellent weapon effective against aircraft, Exocet and even shells. Two Lynx helicopters or one large Sea King helicopter could be carried on deck. Mechanically, the new *Sheffield* would be powered by the same jet engines as the previous ship. Structurally, she would be similarly built, however, much of the material that had burned so fiercely in 1982 was excluded.

Almost exactly two years later, on March 26th 1986, Mrs Susan Stanley, wife of the then Defence Minister, launched the new *Shiny.* Amongst those present were Sam Salt, the last Captain, and relatives of those lost on the second *Sheffield.*

Laying the keel, March 30th 1984.
Peter Jones, the Lord Mayor of Sheffield,
places a specially made coin in the keel
at Swan Hunter's on the Tyne
(Photos: Sheffield Newspapers)

146

During construction in 1985. Above: The superstructure
Below: The Machinery Compartment (Photos: H.M.S.S.A.)

Crew members of Old Shiny in front of New Shiny's bow (Photo: H.M.S.S.A.)

Andrew Stevenson and partner from the City of Sheffield, a survivor of the second HMS Sheffield, at the launch of the third HMS Sheffield
(Photo: Sheffield Newspapers)

The launch. Mrs Susan Stanley starts the third Shiny on her way

Heading down the slipway at 12 knots, to be slowed by a hundred tons of chains, Sheffield enters the water for the first time (Photos: Sheffield Newspapers)

Around twenty *Old Shiny* crew members were also present. For the next couple of years the ship would be fitted out with her electrics, plumbing, weapon systems, air conditioning, bunks, etc.

For the first two *Sheffields,* the bell had been cast by Hadfields. However, by the mid 1980s, Hadfields had closed and so it was down to Edgar Allens, also of Sheffield, to cast the new one. There was to be so much stainless steel on the new ship that her first captain, Nick Barker, proclaimed her the "Shiniest of all the Shiny Sheffs".

Captain Barker had commanded *HMS Endurance* during the Falklands War. It is said that he had warned Whitehall, weeks before the invasion, of Argentina's intentions. His father had commanded *Acasta* that had valiantly defended the aircraft carrier *Glorious* from the German battle cruiser *Scharnhorst* in 1940. *Acasta* was sunk with all hands. The first *Sheffield* had assisted in the sinking of *Scharnhorst* in 1943, but for some reason Nick Barker was relieved of his command of *Sheffield* just days before her commissioning. *Sheffield's* new captain would be Tony Morton, a former Navy pilot. Captain Morton commanded the *Yarmouth* during the Falklands. Sadly, it was the *Yarmouth* which towed the gutted *Sheffield* to her final resting place.

Battle honours plate inscribed with twelve battles of Old Shiny and one from the second HMS Sheffield. The plate also lists the ship's commanders *(Photos: Sheffield Newspapers)*

Footplate cast by Darwins of Templeborough, Rotherham. Commander Tim Emmes takes delivery

The first crew, under the command of Nick Barker (Photo: Crown Copyright/MOD)

March 1988 and, to put it in naval terms, 'In all respects ready for service'
(Photo: Sheffield Newspapers)

The new Sheffield F96 at anchor on the South Coast
(Photo: Crown Copyright/MOD)

The Warship of the 21st Century

Today's *Sheffield* has a similar maximum speed to her predecessor, around thirty knots, or nautical miles per hour. Her two Rolls Royce Olympus gas turbine engines generate 28,000 horse power each. Additionally, the ship is fitted with two smaller Rolls Royce Tyne gas turbine engines which are used for slower, more economical cruising. These smaller engines each generate 5,340 horse power. Both the Olympus and Tyne engines have been developed from aircraft jet engines.

Captain Nick Barker on Sheffield's bridge (Photo: Sheffield Newspapers)

Two propellers and two rudders are fitted and, to steady the ship in rough seas, there are four stabilisers. The ship's electrical power comes from four diesel generators each capable of generating one Mega Watt, enough electricity to supply a small town the size of Bakewell in Derbyshire. The power is distributed throughout the ship on 1500 miles of electric cabling.

Sheffield has a crew of just under three hundred of which around twenty are officers. Junior ratings are accommodated in five mess decks, each having recreation space. Further up the scale, Petty Officers, Chief Petty Officers and Warrant Officers have larger mess decks holding no more than six people.

Sheffield has her own radio and television network complete with a large stock of British television programmes and feature films. Meals are served in two dining rooms, giving two main meals per day with a choice of three main dishes.

In today's Navy the ships are departmentalised. These departments include; Marine Engineering, Supply and Secretarial, Weapons Engineering, Executive, Operations and Air Group.

Firstly, the Marine Engineering Department looks after the engines and generators and, in turn, the electrical power, compressed air, hydraulics,

Fire practice. Crew from the Marine Engineering Department dressed in flameproof overalls and breathing apparatus (Photo: Sheffield Newspapers)

The kitchen (Photo: Sheffield Newspapers)

lighting, heating, air conditioning, fresh water supply and sewage disposal. During combat this department would take care of fire fighting and damage control. Some fifty crew members are employed in this department. Their jobs are highly technical and basically involve knowing every nut and bolt in the ship. Daily maintenance of the ship is also part of their duty.

The Supply and Secretarial Department provides the 'hotel', catering, administrative and stores services to the ship. A Chief Petty Officer is responsible for some 25,000 items of stores, worth over £5 million, ranging from toilet paper to spare parts for missiles. Nearly 800 meals each day are served from the catering section, using a kitchen just three times the size of the average household kitchen. The kitchen bakes its own bread and even produces its own ice cream. Four crew members are employed in the ship's office handling administration, pay, correspondence and records.

Weapons Engineering, as the name suggests, looks after the business end of *Sheffield*. Unlike the *Old Shiny*, where the guns were loaded by hand and shells were sent up from manually loaded magazines, the current *Sheffield* is fully automated. So, the jobs in this department are virtually all electronic. However, the Seawolf missile system is still loaded manually. Around fifty crew members are employed in this section. They are also responsible for the ship's radar and surveillance systems.

The Executive Department is a very diverse area. The Medical Officer looks after the crew's health and the Chief Boatswain's Mate makes sure that everything is always 'shipshape' and ensures that crew members are trained in the art of replenishment at sea.

The civilian manned NAAFI shop selling everything a sailor needs at sea
(Photo: Sheffield Newspapers)

The Physical Training Officer organises *Sheffield's* sporting teams and keeps the crew fit. Written daily orders for the complement are issued by the Routine Office Writer who also ensures that the routines are kept up to date.

The Operations Department is the largest department in today's *Sheffield.* Over one hundred crew members sail the ship, operating radar, sonar, radio and satellite communications and operations for the helicopter.

Every department has its chain of command from Junior ratings, through Senior ratings, to Officers with the Captain taking final responsibility for the whole ship.

Unusual view of Sheffield's stern. The crew is standing on the helicopter deck
(Photo: Sheffield Newspapers)

Firepower

1937: Southampton Class Light Cruiser

*12 six-inch guns in four triple turrets
Range 14 miles*

*8 four-inch guns in four double mount turrets
Range 8 miles*

Two Walrus aircraft can carry anti-submarine depth charges

1975: Type 42, Sheffield Class Guided Missile Destroyer

*A single 4.5 inch gun. Range 14 miles*

Sea Dart anti-aircraft missile system - Range about 40 miles

One Lynx helicopter that can carry anti-submarine torpedoes

1988: Type 22, Broadsword Class Frigate

Four Exocet missiles - Range about 40 miles

Two Sea Wolf anti-missile & anti-aircraft systems - Range less than 10 miles

*Two Lynx helicopters that can carry anti-submarine
torpedoes, or one Sea King helicopter*

GREAT
BRITAIN

EUROPE

NORTH AMERICA

AFRICA

SOUTH AMERICA

Ascension
Island

ARGENTINA

Buenos Aires

Falkland
Islands

Port Stanley

*Areas of action seen
by H.M.S Sheffield*